D0941581

HQ
796.
B36

—REGULATIONS—

FINES ARE CHARGED FOR OVERDUE AND/OR
LOST LIBRARY MATERIALS ... IN ACCOR-
DANCE WITH BOARD ... GRADES
TRANSCRIPTS, DEGREES ... TRATION
PRIVILEGES SHALL BE WIT ... NTIL ALL
LIBRARY BOOKS OR OT ... MATERIALS
ARE RETURNED (TO THE LIBRARY CIRCULATION
DESK)."

Contra Costa College Library
2600 Mission Bell Drive
San Pablo, California 94806

Youth and the Hazards of Affluence

OTHER BOOKS BY GRAHAM B. BLAINE, JR.

Patience and Fortitude: The Parents' Guide to Adolescence
Emotional Problems of the Student (with Charles C. McArthur)

YOUTH and

the HAZARDS

of AFFLUENCE

The High School and College Years

by Graham B. Blaine, Jr., M.D.

Harper & Row, Publishers, New York & London

CONTRA COSTA COLLEGE
DISCARD
SAN PABLO, CALIFORNIA

SEP 2 0 1966
HQ
796
B36

YOUTH AND THE HAZARDS OF AFFLUENCE. *Copyright © 1966 by Graham B. Blaine, Jr. Printed in the United States of America. All rights reserved. No part of this book may be used or reproduced in any manner whatsoever without written permission except in the case of brief quotations embodied in critical articles and reviews. For information address Harper & Row, Publishers, Incorporated, 49 East 33rd Street, New York, N.Y. 10016.*

FIRST EDITION

LIBRARY OF CONGRESS CATALOG CARD NUMBER: 66-15775

C-Q

For CHRISSIE, VICTORIA, AND LILY

Contents

Preface

Cicero raised his arms in horror at the immorality of his contemporaries many centuries ago, crying out, "O tempora! O mores!" Periodically, ever since, the older generation has deplored the behavior of its offspring in phrases such as "They have things too easy" or "What they need is a good kick in the pants."

This book is an attempt to link the present unruly behavior ← of our young people to the general tenor of our times. I hope, also, to point up certain specific factors in our culture which appear to have contributed to this behavior.

Someone was recently quoted as saying, "The first sign of old age is worrying about one's own morals or those of others." But I do not think that I will be called trite or senile by attempting to show that a lack of self-disipline, a tendency toward destructiveness, and a new kind of amorality regarding sex exists among our high school and college students which are unique and deserve analysis. I believe that these changes in attitude and behavior are related to changes in the family, school, and community environment in which today's young people have been raised. Since the last two decades have indeed seen many changes in these cultural areas, it is logical that the behavioral change has been caused to some degree at least by the cultural one.

Over the course of history morals seem to have changed markedly and often. The ribaldry and coarseness of the Restoration comedy seem sharply in contrast to the pretentious strictness and stuffiness of the Victorian era, though there is little evidence that behavior occurring behind the facade was actually very different. It was only talked about differently. Are we today simply encountering a period of greater frankness than ever before, which may soon be abandoned in favor of discreet silence or delicate euphemism as the pendulum swings back in the direction of decorum and politeness? I do not think so. The indications are that a very real change in patterns of behavior, not simply in attitudes, is occurring. It is time to take a careful look, and to evaluate the meaning of the present trend in terms of its effect on future generations as well as on the present one.

I do not mean to derogate affluence. We are fortunate indeed to be in the advantageous economic position we now enjoy. But if there are adjustments to be made in our attitudes toward our children, both as parents and as administrators, then we had best make these adjustments, so that they also can enjoy and be in a position to perpetuate our present happy circumstances.

I wish to express my appreciation here to Mrs. Ruth

Simonds who typed the manuscript and gave invaluable suggestions and encouragement along the way.

Graham B. Blaine, Jr.

Cambridge, Massachusetts
November 1965

Youth and the Hazards of Affluence

CHAPTER 1

Family

More people have more money than ever before. While there remain pockets of poverty in certain isolated rural communities and many shocking slum areas in our cities, almost everywhere else one finds a comfortable affluence unlike that found in any other period of this or any other nation's economic history. Not only in terms of worldly goods, but also in the feelings of prosperity, security, and optimism they experience, the wage earner and homemaker are "wealthier" today. The president of a corporation and the man or woman who sweeps his office are both secure in their belief that they will have a roof over their heads and three meals a day until they die. The uncertainty of the thirties and the inequity of the twenties are no longer with us—nor is the desperateness of the forties when the war years brought sudden tragedy as well as short supply and sacrifice of one kind or another. The fifties and sixties have been years of comparative prosperity. With increasing populations throughout the world, and the developing countries expanding industrially, most Americans feel optimistic about this period of economic abundance continuing into the almost limitless future.

This amount of security and material advantage should offer families ideal physical and emotional conditions for bringing up their children. Tangible goods which enable young people to grow up healthily are easily available, from food and clothing to such nonessential but helpful items as telephones and cosmetics. Psychologically disturbing factors present in the past are absent from almost all homes today. Bankruptcy, eviction, bread lines, and soup kitchens no longer demonstrate to parents and children the precariousness of their economic position. Fear of poverty or of sudden changes in standard of living does not now haunt the mind of the breadwinner and filter down to his children. With this comfortable feeling about the future, with material needs amply supplied, and with so much leisure time available for parent-child good fellowship, our young people should be developing better than ever. With such ideal conditions for healthy nurture our children should be growing into happy, well adjusted young adults, making less trouble for those about them and suffering from less inner turmoil and distress. But are they?

A front page of the *New York Times'* second section picked at random would indicate otherwise. Of eight items on this page, three refer to troubled youth. One headline reads,

2

"Curb on Drinking by Minors Sought"; another, "City Acts to Lock Hydrants and End Abuse by Children," and the third, "Telephone Vandalism Rises; Organized Stealing of Coins by Gangs Plagues Company." This does not appear to be an indicator of a well adjusted younger generation. The main problem represented in these headlines is lack of self-control, and this is the commonest complaint about children today made by teachers, ministers, court workers, and parents themselves (when talking about other people's children). They feel that most of these problems stem from a lack of self-discipline, and a degree of selfishness which is unbelievable to adults who themselves respect the rights of others and think of them before acting.

Self-discipline does not grow like Topsy, but is the result of a two-stage building process in which parents are the prime movers. Church, school, peers, and heroes play a part, too, but it is at home that the cornerstone is laid.

The subsequent chapters in this book will deal exclusively with problems encountered by parents, schools, and colleges in their relationships with adolescents and young adults; but the early years at home leave such an important mark that some description of these background influences must be included here. Otherwise the variations in the reactions of individual high school and college students to the multiple temptations and opportunities offered them cannot begin to be explained or understood. Attitudes and behavior of eighteen-year-olds are controlled to a considerable degree by an internal gyroscope which was formed and set during the years before ten, and their actions should not be judged without knowledge of this mechanism and the extent of its effect.

Consideration for others, altruism, & remorse cannot be expected from young men and women whose childhood experience lacked the necessary precursors for the development of such attributes.

THE DEVELOPMENT OF CONSCIENCE

During early childhood (one to seven) the conscience begins to develop, and though it never is incapable of change, the degree to which it can be influenced varies considerably with age. In the early years a basic underlayer is formed which guides and controls feelings and action then and for life. If the opportunity to help in the development of this vital underpinning is neglected or mishandled by parents during these years, there is no way to make up for it later. The young child is able to absorb into his self-regulating apparatus the prohibitions and restrictions of his parents and to make them a part of his permanent and irrevocable inner self. The parents' ability to influence their child's future is never again so great, and it cannot be emphasized too strongly how important it is for them to be aware of this fact and to be conscientious about fulfilling their obligation to their children at this time and in this respect. Individuals who have not, as children, had limits firmly set upon their impulsive behavior by clear disapproval, spanking, or deprivation, and who have not been shown that the outside world is a force to be reckoned with—rather than a boundless, limitless, undefined emptiness—will not be able to control their impulses. At times they may be carried to extremes of achievement and productivity by the energy contained in these impulses, but at other

4

times they will cause great suffering to others by following destructive desires of their own. At still other periods of their lives they may be paralyzed because of their inability to marshal sufficient will power and strength of resolve to overcome the regressive pull toward indolence and lethargy common to all human beings. Willingness to punish, and firmness of conviction about what is right and wrong, are essential qualities in the good parent. Sometimes they may be missing in one parent and present in the other. This seems to make little difference as long as one sets the limits clearly, firmly, and consistently in those early years during which the first stages of conscience formation occur.

A second stage for parents occurs when a child is about ten or twelve, and should be marked principally by a change from limit setting to example setting, combined with a willingness to allow children in these early adolescent years to learn by experience. At this time prohibitions are resented and rebelled against by children. The moment is past when attitudes can be deeply incorporated into the basic core of the personality through direct command. Rules for living can no longer be learned by a wish to avoid the pain of punishment. However, without being aware of it the older child can take on as a part of himself what he admires most about those in his environment whom he respects. Parents, teachers, and relatives become models, and though he does not usually imitate them outright he unconsciously adopts characteristics here and there from many. Most essential at this time is a "shift of gears" for parents. They should continue to define clearly their views on ethical, religious, and political matters but not insist on conformity with these views. The adolescent needs to know where his elders stand, and they should clarify their character for his benefit; but then they should allow him unconsciously to pick and choose whatever elements, from whomever's character, he is to absorb into his own personality.

Adolescence is the period when the underlying core of conscience laid down in the early years is most needed. This is a time of necessary rebellion—when superimposed values seem fake and artificial. The individual self becomes all-important, and the search for what comes truly from within and therefore seems real is a consuming task. It involves experimenting with new ideas, new ways of behavior, and different ways of dressing, and the trying out of new goals and ambitions; but always as the limiter of action there remains the basic core of conscience provided by childhood training from the parents, which prevents completely self-defeating or self-destructive behavior. This core of conscience does need some reinforcing, however, during adolescence. Parents and schools still must show by their rules and restrictions that they will not tolerate infractions of certain basic principles such as those relating to sex, alcohol, and crime. They cannot totally abdicate their role as a potential source of pain and punishment, but in general this role must be reserved for major issues.

Modern Obstacles to Conscience Formation

Many American parents are failing their children at both stages of the two-stage operation which brings about the attainment of self-discipline and will power. Permissive methods of teaching and training were introduced in the early decades of this century, and their influence on parents and schools has been tremendous. Misinterpreting and extrapolating from some of Freud's early theorizings, some educators and psychologists became convinced that restricting a child's emotions or actions would cause dangerous inhibitions to be built up which would in turn cause serious neurosis later in life. This led them to advise parents and teachers to stop punishing children and instead encourage them to insult and fight each other as their spirit or psyche moved them. Furthermore, these innovators felt that destructive behavior should be tolerated and even encouraged as a way to rid the developing personality of aggression and prevent the formation of such symptoms as frigidity, ritualistic behavior, and the tension illnesses (high blood pressure, peptic ulcer, and palpitation). Children's energies, they contended, should not be channeled into working at tasks which appeared unpleasant to the child, for fear that this too would lead to a building up of repressed anger and resentment which would cause a damming up of originality and creativity. Schools were encouraged to watch their pupils for signs of spontaneous interest and then to encourage these to the exclusion of the classic three R's.

Freud did indeed relate certain symptoms he found in ill individuals to extreme control exerted by rigid parents, but he never postulated that all the world would be better off without discipline. To say that because some people develop emotional illness as a result of over-restriction in childhood, all forms of restriction are harmful, is as absurd as reaching the conclusion that no one should swim because some people suffer colds in the head after having wet feet. The unfortunate consequences of the permissive method became apparent in the late thirties and early forties. The free-for-all play-grounds which called themselves schools were out of style and out of business by the beginning of World War II, but the attitude toward children engendered by this misguided experiment has died slowly. Dr. Spock and many others who are widely read and deeply respected have pointed out clearly and strongly the urgent need for discipline and for limit setting in early childhood; yet in many homes these words are little heeded.

Adult Americans do not usually cling to fads when they have been proved harmful or have become unpopular with doctors and other respected professionals. It seems uncharacteristic for them to continue to abdicate their responsibility as disciplinarians in the face of such strong advice to the contrary. Part of the reason, perhaps, for this reluctance to return to the child-rearing practices that had endured so long is the present reliance on automation which has led to a "hands off" attitude. So much is done automatically nowadays that it is easy to see how parents might assume a child's internal clockwork will click along providing the right ingredients for him at the proper moment, and shifting from soak, to rinse, to spin dry when each of these particular procedures is necessary. Of course when the door flies open and the product comes out less than perfect, consternation reigns and criticisms fly—the latter often unjustifiably directed against the school which is expected to iron out the kinks and take out the dirt as the family had failed to do. But mid-adolescence is too late to wake up and realize that there had never been an automatic device regulating the growth of the child in the first place. There are no teaching machines that can replace the parents.

8

No box with dials, lights, or hearing elements can do the job that must be done early. There is no mechanical substitute for the rewards of parents' hugs, smiles, glows of pride, nor for the punishments felt from a frown, growl, spanking, or groan of disappointment. Human communication by voice, hand, facial expression, or loving arms is as essential for healthy child development as air and water.

THE COMMUNICATION BREAKDOWN

It is in this latter area, communication or the lack of it, that we find another increasingly detrimental factor in the bringing up of our children. Our present affluence plays a part here, for as more jobs are available for women, there are fewer hours when mothers are available to communicate with their children. Fathers, too, who spend little enough time at home under any circumstances, now often have two jobs and are asleep almost every moment they are in the house. There has been much talk about the increase in leisure time, but statistics show that the American male is a restless soul and a greedy one. Overtime and moonlighting occupy more of his new "leisure" time than any other occupation—recreation or just relaxing with the family included. One cannot discourage employment opportunities and advocate an increase in unemployment in order to bring families together, but greater attention should be paid to the necessity for conversational and emotional exchange between children and their parents.

Another important factor which inhibits intrafamilial communication is television viewing. Much has been made of the influence of television programs on the thinking and character

9

development of our young people. Although most critics agree that the quality of the shows is poor, nothing much seems to come of this criticism. Actually, it is not so much what is seen that is damaging as the divisive influence of the watching itself. In many homes mealtime is the only time for conversation and for mutual exchange of ideas and attitudes. Yet in some households the television set is placed in the kitchen or TV dinners are carried to the set. No member of the family ever comes to know what any of the others are thinking or doing. A recent cartoon, too close to the truth to be funny, showed husband and wife looking at a television screen which displayed the words: "Network trouble. Stand by." Husband says to wife, "So how have you been this week?"

Not only does television distract from family communication, but it also physically separates children from parents, for in many homes there are two sets, one for parents and one for children. When children fight with each other, feel bored, or are perplexed about some personal situation and ask for advice, it is all too easy for parents to say "Whyn't you go look at TV?" instead of trying to get at the root of the problem. Fathers are hypnotized by marathon baseball and football programs, and children tell time by the appearance of favorite shows. The television set is an invader in the home which is here to stay; but it can be utilized in ways that are healthy and contributory rather than unhealthy and disruptive.

OVERABUNDANCE OF MATERIAL THINGS

When it comes to the second stage of conscience development—that which takes place during the adolescent years—affluence has undermined parental influence by making material goods generally and easily available; and it has affected the growing child by depriving him of the opportunity to meet a truly satisfying challenge.

Here we can employ a principle of Freud's to good effect. It was he who defined maturity as the ability to postpone gratification. He pointed out that small children live by what he called the pleasure principle, demanding immediate gratification of every wish and not able to undergo any degree of present discomfort in order to gain greater pleasure at a later moment. The mature adult learns to think in long range terms. He can endure frustration and spend long hours working hard to attain an end worth the effort expended and more satisfying than the nothing that would have come from doing nothing. In America today, however, the luxuries are in good supply and for a large part of our population the means to obtain them are right at hand—if not through instalment buying, then by an instant loan pressed by a generous local bank or the "Friendly" or "Beneficial" loan company just around the corner. Few parents now can set a good example for their children in the art of saving or of sacrificing the pleasure of the moment for more gratifying enjoyments in the future.

Most children cannot logically and honestly be deprived of what they think they need, even though the individual items may seem to their parents trivial and far from necessary. Bicycles, personal radios, private telephones, and automobiles need no longer be earned by taking jobs but instead can be paid for out of the family income, stretched as it so easily is by borrowing on future earnings. Even the satisfactions and risks of running away from home have been minimized by the collect telephone call and the telegraphed money order which rescue the runaway as soon as the going gets tough. Young men and women have a hard time finding a testing ground for their powers of endurance, physical strength, or frustration tolerance.

This is not to say that we must start a war or force a depression, but rather that we should learn how to provide our children with what they need for healthy personality development without depriving them of the obvious advantages that have come to them in this era of economic abundance. Ways in which this can be done will be discussed in later chapters.

While few of today's young people remember Hiroshima, its horror is vividly enough recaptured in photographs and films to bring home to all of them its moment of sudden and massive killing. Also, many of them were witness to the temporary hysteria of a few years ago when air raid drills were conducted routinely in schools, and bomb shelters were being promoted and sold. At some level of consciousness, the high school and college student recognizes that the possibility of total annihilation is frighteningly real and that his hopes and ambitions could be snuffed out by the push of a button thousands of miles away. How much does this realization influence his ability to apply himself to studies or to struggle for advancement in his job or career?

This is a difficult question to answer, for young people do not often seriously discuss with their elders or in the papers, articles, and books they write this cloud which hangs over them. When it does come up, it is often in the form of a macabre or "sick" joke. Children, for instance, during the days of scheduled bomb drills used to ask each other, "What

are you going to be when you blow up?" and during the great
Eastern power blackout college students asked, "Have you
heard from Moscow lately? Maybe the message is on the
way."

Such banter may represent a false bravado which thinly
covers a great deal of anxiety; and both the apathy and rebellion, which will be discussed later in this book, may be mani-
festations of this anxiety. Still, there is little concrete evidence
to support such a hypothesis. Reported dreams and psychological tests, such as the Rorschach (inkblot) test, both give
evidence of unconscious preoccupations, and atomic explosions
do not appear in test results often enough to indicate that fears
of imminent destruction play a significant part in the average
person's adjustment to the world around him. Perhaps the
relative impermanence of our civilization contributes a little
to the cavalier or "cool" attitude of some of today's college
students, but in most it seems to be a fear so deeply buried that
it could interfere only slightly with their conscientiousness
and long-range planning.

The recent escalation of the Vietnam war does appear, however, to have had a psychological effect on the American
college student. His readiness to become violent and destructive seems less and his willingness to express loyalty to his
country has come more to the fore. It has been noted by many
observers that suicides and other forms of violence occur far
less frequently during wartime. Perhaps our normal aggressive-
ness gains a vicarious outlet when the nation is at war, or perhaps it is because individuals know that they can find an
honorable arena in which to act out their hostilities. Also,
when the country is in trouble, those who are in revolt against

"the establishment" tend to bury their resentments temporarily in order to help preserve the elements in the present order in which they believe and which may be threatened. It is reassuring now to find that since the Vietnam war has expanded, there have been almost as many students demonstrating in support of government policies in Vietnam as there have been students demonstrating against these policies. In addition, the nature of student protest itself, whether it be against national or university policy, has recently been of a less destructive and less violent nature.

THE EFFECTS OF DIVORCE

One corollary of failure to postpone gratification and to tolerate frustration in the service of a greater good is the startlingly high divorce rate in this country. The divorce rate here is double that of any other country in the world. Many factors are responsible for this, but one is probably the prevalent attitude that action should be taken if a marriage relationship is less than ideal. The unrealistic concept of romantic love which is more popular here than in other countries also plays a part. It fosters the belief that marriages are made in heaven and leads some spouses to think that if the idyllic love of the courtship does not continue, then he or she simply married the wrong person and should back up and try again. More important is the current feeling that one is entitled to a "happy" marriage and that the best way to achieve it is through switching partners rather than going through a comparatively complicated and often troubling period of adjustment with its agonizing, unpleasant reappraisals and compromises. The quick solution provided by divorce may be helpful to the emotional equilibrium of the parents but it seldom does the same for their children. Certain guiding principles about divorce can be described with reasonable assurance as a result of a number of careful sociological and psychological studies conducted over the past few years.

Children, no matter how much they may feign indifference and lack of concern regarding their parents' separation, cannot emerge from divorce unscathed. There are times, however, when the trauma inflicted upon the children by the continuation of a marriage would be greater than that brought about by a divorce, provided that the placement of the children is carefully considered and carried out.

Children, particularly those younger than ten, can put up with more family discord without being distressed than most adults realize. Arguments and disputes, even heated ones, can be overheard and observed by children dispassionately. They can be quite objective about such controversies, and even discuss them humorously among themselves. Anger and frustration are emotions with which they are familiar, and watching such feelings being openly expressed by their elders may even be reassuring.

But threats of separation or divorce are another story. One of the most powerful unconscious fears harbored by a child is that he will be deserted and abandoned by one or both parents. To have this frightening fantasy made real by hearing his mother or father talk about leaving may be deeply disturbing. When a couple cannot refrain from threatening one another with divorce so openly that it is obvious to the children, either directly or by implication, then a separation which will bring some security and consistency into the family pattern should be seriously considered. A situation even more difficult for young children to withstand without harm is for one parent angrily to walk out for a time and then return unexpectedly, only to repeat the performance a few months later. Children can understand parents' not getting along perfectly all the time (they have the same problem), but permanent disruption of the family unit is something they are unable to comprehend. The constant threat of such an event can be worse than the reality.

Alcoholism and physical violence are also factors that upset and damage children. Loss of control in a physical sense, or as a result of intoxication, causes fear in the young because of its unpredictability. Disputes can become a kind of routine, with a foreseeable beginning, middle, and end, but this is not true when blows are struck. Children say with genuine fear in their voices, "I didn't know what was going to happen next." Then, too, there is the embarrassment that accompanies alcoholism, which makes children unwilling to have friends over and causes them to become isolated and withdrawn at a time when companionship is very important.

AGES WHEN DIVORCE IS LESS DAMAGING

If it becomes clear, for whatever reason, that divorce is inevitable, then the question of how long to hold off may arise. It may be possible to keep a marriage functioning until the children are at an age when they will be less affected. In general, divorce or separation does not register with much impact from infancy through the age of three. Very young children are not aware of sex differences and do not have a need for a distinctively masculine person to any significant degree. As long as the child under three stays with its mother, it will probably not be seriously affected emotionally by the absence of its father.

From three to six, however, the child needs both parents more than at any other period. Intimate feelings toward the parent of the opposite sex occur at this stage of development, and these feelings need to be diluted and modified by counteracting feelings about the other parent. It is very difficult for a child to develop normal attitudes toward others later in life if during this three-to-six interval in his growth he does not have both a mother and a father with whom to interact. This is one of the most traumatic periods for a child to lose a parent through death or divorce.

During the next phase, from six to twelve, there is less need for the presence of both parents, and a shift of the adult figures in a child's life is tolerated better. A process of reconciliation with and imitation of the parent of the same sex is beginning at this time, and if a choice must be made about placement with one parent, the presence of the parent of the same sex is preferable unless he or she is a particularly inadequate person.

Adolescents from twelve to eighteen can usually understand the necessity of divorce or separation, and therefore may not suffer as much as younger children, except when the result is the loss of the parent of the same sex. During adolescence, the most important task to be accomplished is the formation of an independent and individual identity. For this to take place successfully, the presence of a strong and effective person of the same sex in the close emotional environment is essential. This can be a stepfather, stepmother, family retainer who has distinctive characteristics, a tutor, an uncle, or an aunt who is living in the home. If this sort of identification figure cannot be included in the plans for the placement of a twelve- to eighteen-year-old, then divorce should be postponed if at all possible.

CUSTODY OF CHILDREN AFTER DIVORCE

Once divorce is definitely decided upon, the custody arrangements for the children usually become a major issue. In determining what is best, a good deal depends on whether or not one parent is going to remarry immediately. Long range psychological studies of individuals followed from infancy to middle age have shown that the two factors most crucial to normal development are: first, the presence of an adult man and woman in the home for relatively lengthy periods (it is not necessary that they be the actual parents, nor is it essential that they be the same two adults during the entire childhood and adolescent period); second, a place which can be felt as home. This may be one small room or an estate, but it should be as permanent as possible and represent to the child a spot where he can always go—a sanctuary where his own private possessions are, a refuge which keeps away the rootless, floating feeling that can be so terrifying to a youngster. Nobody feels more lost than the ten-year-old who has no answer to the question, "Where do you live?" Yet, to have to reply "Des Moines and Boston" may be even worse than "Nowhere."

Providing for each child what comes closest to fulfilling these two requirements should be the primary goal. Boarding school often seems to be the easiest and most appropriate solution, but for children under twelve it rarely turns out to be successful. More individual adult attention is needed at this age than can be provided by the average boarding school. Teachers may seem to be excellent parent surrogates, but the siblings in such a school are too numerous and too needful themselves to allow any one student the degree and depth of relationship he needs.

A psychiatrist tells of one patient who, because of a divorce in his family, had been sent to boarding school from the age of nine until college. At twenty-five he still perceived his older friends and associates as schoolteachers or housemasters, believing them to be constantly checking up on him and pleased only when they had caught him in some error. Authority had been a distant and exclusively disciplinary force for so long during his important formative years that he could not envision it as possibly being constructively critical, friendly, or willing to accept him as an individual. This misconception regarding the amount of hostility in the world at large had led to the personality clashes at work and in his marriage which brought him to seek treatment. Firm but friendly discipline, coupled with complete acceptance, must be part of the upbringing of children younger than twelve, and the atmosphere at the ordinary boarding school does not provide it.

The "six-and-six split" (six months with each parent) would seem on the surface to be the fairest arrangement, but it has many pitfalls. In the first place, it is hard to feel at home in any house that is lived in only half the year. Roots that have to be pulled up so often rarely go down and spread out enough to provide stability and growth. Also, all too often the children are used unintentionally as pawns in a complicated power struggle between divorced husband and wife. Each parent may try to outdo the other in currying favor with the children, and, worst of all, one may depreciate the other in the eyes of the children because of bitterness and antagonism held over from the days before the divorce.

There are often complications about means and cost of transportation from one establishment to another, as well as bickering about just when is the most convenient time for each parent to have the children. In the end, the child is frequently left with the feeling that he is a victim of vindictiveness and is valued only for his ability to spy on one parent for the other. Finally, there is the financial pressure, for the child may come to feel that he is only a source of funds for mother and a troublesome expense for father.

A student who had been subjected to this kind of divided living came for treatment because of deep depression at the time of the Christmas holidays during his sophomore year at prep school. He had always experienced mild feelings of discouragement at vacation time, but this year it was worse. His depression turned out to be linked to the fact that, for completely unrelated reasons, neither parent wanted to have him home for Christmas. His mother was going to her second husband's family, and his father was planning a honeymoon cruise with his third wife. The boy had to face up to the fact that for many years he had had no one place he could call home. He had been consciously bothered all along, but until this moment of rejection by both sides of his family he had not realized the depth of his loneliness. Perhaps it was as well that events turned out as they did, for the severe depression led him to seek psychiatric help and eventually to become better reconciled to his situation.

Living under the year-round custody of one parent, with flexible visiting privileges with the other, would seem to have many advantages over the six-and-six split, but here, too, there are snags. Principal among these is the danger of forcing too much responsibility on a child too young—depriving him of the carefree pleasures that should make up such a large part of the years from three to twelve.

This occurs most often when a child is placed with the parent of the opposite sex, either alone or with younger brothers and sisters. Then a boy takes on the role of man of the house, shares in decision making, helps discipline the younger children, and later may even serve as mother's escort on social occasions. This not only tends to make a sobersides out of him, but also ties him emotionally to his mother in a way that may seriously interfere with his forming relationships with women his own age throughout life. Likewise, a girl living with her father can quickly adopt a wifelike attitude—preparing meals, cleaning the house, and perhaps playing hostess when friends come in. This can age her before her time and cause her to be permanently uninterested in the activities and dating customs of her contemporaries.

Tragic results can be caused by this kind of placement, as was true in the case of a high school senior who committed suicide after running away from his mother's home to his father's place in the South. This boy's parents were divorced when he was fifteen, and against his wishes arrangements were made for him to live with his mother and three younger sisters. He took his responsibilities toward them very seriously, but his schoolwork and his dating relationships did not go well. Several short stays with his father only strengthened the boy's feelings of admiration and respect for him, and the separation became even more intolerable. When a last desperate plea to the father for a chance to live with him was turned down, the boy decided that life was not worth while.

Children over twelve should have elders of their own sex, whom they admire, close to them so that they may identify with them, take advantage of their advice, and follow their example. Generally speaking, isolating a child from his brothers and sisters works out badly. Children like to discuss their concerns with each other. They need the reassurance which comes from finding that another shares their feelings and that they are not alone in experiencing confusion, loneliness, and resentment over what has happened. No real harm comes from sending siblings in groups of two or more to separate homes, although care should be taken to keep together twins, or children close in age or feeling for each other.

As a rule it is not a good idea to give children a choice in regard to the parent with whom they will live. Often they are afraid of offending one parent, or of punishment if they do not say what they think a harsh parent wants to hear. A child's choice made out of fear is less likely to be right than one made by parents or advisers out of their wisdom and experience. In most situations it is best to have the placement of the children firmly decided upon before they are told about the divorce. An interim of uncertainty during which parents, lawyers, and grandparents bicker over what is best for the children makes them feel unwanted and afraid of being abandoned. This can lead to serious guilt and depression.

When a child becomes an adult, he sees the people around him with the same eyes with which he saw his parents. His view of men and women will always be influenced by what he saw in his father and mother or those who substituted for them as he grew up. If these significant adults were inconsistent, untrustworthy, unreliable, and deceitful, he will always suspect that the same characteristics lie hidden in all men and women, whether or not there is outward evidence of them in day-to-day behavior.

Because children's views of their parents are so vitally important in their future orientation to the world at large, the single most important mistake to avoid in situations involving divorce is the depreciation by one parent of the other in the presence of children. If this undermining course is avoided, and the other principles outlined above are followed, particularly the making of a home and the presence in it of a healthy adult of the same sex, then the chances of normal development taking place are excellent, despite the separation of parents. The children of such a carefully and unselfishly planned divorce can expect to achieve satisfying relationships with their peers and to avoid repeating their parents' mistakes when they face difficulties in their own marriages later in life.

In summary, then, parents must provide certain attitudes and clear examples if they wish their children to develop normally. Positive definition of the limits of acceptable and unacceptable behavior in early childhood, models of an identifiable sort which demonstrate the advantages of delayed gratification, and encouragement to test out strength and abilities through meeting real challenges during adolescence—these are the bare bones of what is needed. Combined with them, of course, should be open lines of communication freely available, and an atmosphere of love and acceptance that outlasts all of the tests and provocations at which the young are so adept.

CHAPTER 2

Education

Our present affluence has brought extensive education within the reach of nearly all young people, either directly or indirectly through scholarship funds or aid from private and government grants. Learning, along with gaining opportunity to pursue it, forms the core of existence from the age of five until twenty-five. Although only about 35 per cent will actually stay in school until that age, the possibility of doing so, the consequences of not having done so, or the attempt to do so occupies the minds of most of the rest as well. At times this country appears to be obsessed by the concept of education and to have made a fetish of it. This must perplex observers from Europe, where higher education is reserved for the scholar and the professional. Here it is deemed so precious and so essential that it is foisted upon many who appear to have no natural desire or aptitude for it.

This is a relatively recent phenomenon, for in 1900 only 10 per cent of our high school graduates went on to college—a figure very close to the present European proportion. Now approximately 55 per cent enter college, of whom 45 to 55 per cent drop out at least once during their four years. This represents a nationwide average which runs higher in the state universities where, in some instances, well over 50 per cent of the freshmen each year find college not up to their expectation or beyond their capability.

The common European practice of qualifying examinations given to students of ten to fourteen years of age may seem unfair and does probably discriminate against some "late bloomers," but it succeeds in taking the pressure off students in their last years of high school. Those who fall into the 90 per cent category for whom the possibility of higher education is eliminated can prepare themselves for immediate jobs or trades, and are subjected to a far less rigorous academic schedule than those who have qualified for a university education. The subject matter of their courses in school may not be as sophisticated, but the relaxed manner in which they can approach them undoubtedly leads to more permanent retention, with greater usefulness later in the vocation they eventually choose to pursue.

Those who qualify for higher education may continue under less pressure also, since they now have considerable assurance that they will be given an opportunity to continue their education beyond high school. The year of the qualifying exam is a pressured one, and there has been criticism of this allegedly inhumane method of culling the talented from the less so. Still, an early and a quick decision has many advantages over the prolonged pressure to excel which is exerted on the American high school student today from parents, teachers, and business firms.

In his book, *The Sheepskin Psychosis*, John Keats quotes a private survey of industrial personnel officers which indicated that most businesses today require a college education for no logical reason but simply as a convenient screening device.

In most countries, a university liberal arts education is not a requirement for success in industry or politics but is reserved for professional men and scholars. It seems sensible to make higher education available to all who are interested in expanding their general knowledge, whether or not this expansion is later used directly in their careers. Ideally, students should be free to choose education beyond high school to satisfy their own intellectual curiosity provided they are intelligent enough to do so; but those who do not enjoy learning for its own sake, and who do not plan professional or highly technical careers, probably should not be forced by families, schools, or irrational screening customs into beginning a college experience they have no stomach for.

Causes of Underachievement

We are living in times which make college education both a rite and a right. We cannot do what would appear to most to be a setting back of the clock by limiting opportunity for higher education. Instead we must cope with all the complicated problems that expanding the scope of education has brought us. The first of these is a tremendous increase in the number of students who are underachieving. High school counselors as well as psychiatrists and child guidance clinics report a growing tide of parents bringing in children who are not "living up to their potential," and college psychiatrists report that the most frequent complaint in their offices is that of an inability to study or to concentrate.

Since we in America have committed ourselves to providing higher education for a substantial majority of our high school students, we must understand the causes for the inability of many of these educationally privileged young men and women to make use of their opportunity. For an increasingly large proportion of those in school their intellect is only partially available. Despite good intentions and long hours expended, learning simply does not take place. As the students themselves put it, "My wheels are spinning" or "The college experience is going right through me and out the other side" or "Nothing registers." Even if we eliminate those who truly do not want to be in school or college, and those who are there with only a status motive and no intellectual curiosity, we are still left with a large number of intelligent, well motivated, conscientious students whose achievement is blocked by sabotaging mechanisms that interfere with learning. What are these sabotaging mechanisms?

One can be described as the impression that studying is being done in an emotional vacuum. This cause of underachievement is more prevalent in the larger schools where the student-faculty ratio gives little opportunity for teachers to voice individual praise or appreciation. Parents who are remote geographically or emotionally can also be part of the cause. A former dean at Colby tells the story of a sophomore who came to him at the time of leaving college because he was disheartened by his academic performance. The dean asked the young man to send postcards back during his trip to California to look for a job, and hoped he would soon return. The student drove only twenty miles before turning back and going to the dean to say, "I've decided to stay. I didn't know that anyone around here cared enough to ask for a postcard."

Parents who are out of touch with their children, or who seem to care only about their own prestige in relation to their son's success, also run the risk of contributing to a lack of effectiveness in studying. One mother put a golden "A" on her bracelet whenever her son achieved one in school, and thus built up crippling resentment in the boy. He felt this to be a selfish stealing of his glory, and developed severe anxiety before exams until this resentment was understood and expressed in the course of psychiatric treatment. Another college junior became seriously emotionally disturbed when his family were all out of reach by letter or phone for an eight-week period.

Feedback from parents or school and sometimes both is often a prerequisite for academic performance that equals potential. While grades and rank in class may be rewards sufficient in themselves for the ordinary student, in the case of many others personal interest which provides emotional feedback from an individual and not simply from an institution is needed.

Of the many forms adolescent rebellion may take, underachievement is probably the most subtle and insidious. Subtle because it is rarely recognized for what it is by student, parent, or school; and insidious because it often begins in such a quiet fashion that it may not be recognized or treated as rebellion until too late to save a promising career from being delayed or even destroyed. What is so commonly termed laziness, lack of will power, or poor attitude is at heart often a sullen resentfulness expressed by a stubborn refusal to do anything demanded by authority. Most students suffering from this rebelliousness do not themselves realize that they have hostile feelings against authority, and admit it only after it is shown to them. This is often done by pointing out that in almost everything they do they are acting defiantly, either passively by not doing simple chores or leaving their rooms a mess, or actively by behavior such as breaking the speed limit or stealing street signs. Only then do they begin to see that, unconsciously, they are retaliating against their parents by flunking out of school. Once the reality of their action is apparent, its irrationality becomes clearly evident and some attempts to alter behavior may begin.

Schools and parents unwittingly reinforce rather than counteract unconscious feelings of resentment by taking overly punitive attitudes toward students doing disappointingly in their studies. Withdrawal of privileges to make more time for study often simply provokes more rage, and actual time spent in effective study ends up being far less. This is a particularly unwise practice in the case of athletics, for here the additional element of removing a healthy outlet for rebellion is present. Not only is a pleasurable form of activity which often brings with it an encouraging feeling of competence eliminated, but also the student is deprived of an opportunity to kick out, run out, or bat out some of his powerful aggressive impulses in a constructive manner. Instead, these feelings must be contained within where they may become turned against the person himself in the form of depression and self-hate, or expressed indirectly outward as a further inability to cooperate with or obey authority.

Another underlying cause for underachievement is a basic sense of inferiority that persists despite tests and occasional performance which may testify to superior ability. Deeply rooted in some individuals is a strong fear of meeting an accurate test of ability. As long as a total effort toward accomplishing a given assignment is not expended, the result is not felt to be a true test of capability. Such an individual would feel naked and exposed without an excuse to explain away the failure that he expects will result even after a wholehearted effort. This, too, is an unconscious feeling and an exceedingly difficult one to bring to the surface or to resolve. It is more likely to play a part in underachievement in students who are low in the sibling rank order. The children who come along late in the family tend to feel inferior. They find themselves constantly trying to catch up with their older brothers and sisters and they can never quite make it. When they are very young, they are unable to understand that their constant disappointment results from being younger rather than from any actual physical or intellectual deficiency. Often they develop an inner expectation of defeat which inhibits their willingness to compete even when the odds appear heavily in their favor.

Separating and individualizing brothers or sisters to cut down on the amount of competitive activity between them helps prevent problems with underachievement later on. At the high school and college levels, ungraded courses and un-ranked classes can encourage a student's personal interests and thereby build up confidence. As a result he may lose his fear of competing, be able for the first time to make a total effort, and give up reliance on the excuse of not having tried.

Finally, as a basic cause for poor results in study there may be an underlying fear of success. Some students prefer the comparative anonymity of the middle of the class to an atten-tion attracting spot on the honor roll. Such individuals tend to be shy and retiring. In some cases they feel secretly guilty and may be afraid of exposure. Such reasons for avoiding the lime-light may be quite unknown to the student but be active beneath his level of awareness. A person who is afraid of aggression may prefer not to incur the envy of others by excelling. The bright boy of the class may be teased as a "greasy grind" or hated because he is the object of so much praise. For individuals who want to be everybody's friend, this can be a very uncomfortable position and one to be avoided rather than striven for. This fear of success may be deeply hidden, and students whose studying is interfered with for this reason often need extensive counseling to overcome their difficulty.

Obviously, not all underachievers have become such be-cause of the present wide availability of educational opportu-nity and the pressure on every student to push ahead as far and as fast as he can; but these factors do play a significant part in the over-all set of the student today. Family prestige, school and family pressure to study harder, a high degree of competitiveness for grades and admission, and in many instances considerable notoriety when success is achieved lie in the background of the school and college experience for most students today, and all of these elements have been shown to contribute to underachievement.

The School and College Dropout

Often a result, or at least a corollary, of underachievement is dropping out of school or college. Much attention has recently been focused on this act, and much of the alarm expressed about it would seem unwarranted, for a very high percentage of dropouts return to continue their education at their original institution or another. This proportion, indeed, is so great that one educator at a recent symposium about college dropouts remarked that "the only true dropout is a dead dropout." Although many who leave high school before graduation do not return, and employment for such untrained individuals is becoming more and more of a problem in our complicated technological labor market, most end up in an apprenticeship of some sort. Until trade and vocational schools become more plentiful and more respected, such on-the-job training is the only alternative for the high school dropout who does not return to school.

Most students who gain admission to college do not permanently remove themselves from the educative process when they drop out. For a large majority it is only a temporary respite. When they do return to study or training, they do so with greater enthusiasm and considerably more energy.

The principal advantage of interrupting an education lies in

33

breaking out of a rut, leading from pre-nursery school through graduate school, dug not by the student but by others for him. He feels pushed from behind along this rut, and not pulled by what lies ahead nor driven from within by personal need or present satisfaction. At Harvard about 25 per cent of the original 1,200 admitted as freshmen leave college sometime before the four years are over. About 80 per cent of these students return and complete their education eventually at Harvard, and most of the others pursue further education elsewhere.

Dropping out of school can be a helpful and a healthy occurrence for underachievers, not only because it allows them to break out of a rut but also because it often enables them to perform tasks, either at a job or in the armed services, which are relatively simple but are definite and completable. Many school assignments are vague and not capable of being done totally. For an apprehensive or perfectionistic student they may cause a constant anxiety. Often a dropout who is engaged in a simple task, such as programming a computer or digging a garden, will comment on the pleasure of seeing the fruit of his labor right in front of him rather than being left wondering whether enough of the just-read book is in his head to enable him to pass tomorrow's exam. Then, too, receiving cold cash in hot hand every Friday is a pleasant feeling and has many advantages over a mere grade—so intangible, substanceless, and unmarketable. The pleasure of seeing a job done well and done completely, and the receipt of payment in return, can lead to an increased feeling of competence and mastery that is translated later, on return to school, into a more confident and conscientious approach to assigned work.

For still other students a period of time away from school

34

serves as a way to gain perspective. Many young men and women tend to feel at some point in their lives that everything their parents put value on is worthless. It is not until they see for themselves that they cannot gain respect or advancement without education that these students can understand the reason for continuing in school. Many of them feel alien in the world of the day laborer which looked so attractive from inside the schoolhouse walls. They find that such an environment is not compatible, and are glad to return to the company of those with intellectual interests who now seem somehow much more congenial and less "square."

The advantages inherent in interrupting the educational process have been recognized by at least two highly respected organizations, Yale University and the Carnegie Corporation. The president of the former, Kingman Brewster, announced that in 1966 an experimental program financed by the Carnegie Corporation would send some Yale juniors abroad not to study but rather to work in the developing countries. In explaining the reason for believing that this type of program would be helpful to certain students, Brewster said:

The unbroken prospect of competitively driven conventional academic achievement from age five to twenty-five breaks the motivation of many of the most highly motivated and dulls the intellectual enthusiasms of some of the most intelligent . . . to the considerable number of the young who yearn to become involved in something more meaningful than inherited patterns of success, learning too often seems to be involvement's adversary.

The feelings of the dropout have never been more eloquently described. Our attention undoubtedly is better directed toward encouragement of the dropout's return to education than toward prevention of his leaving in the first place.

Most students make more effective use of the school experience if they have a chance to view it from outside rather than only from within.

THE EDUCATION OF WOMEN

Discussion about educating women has been heard loud and long over the years, but today it has special relevance. For not only have women invaded more and more of men's occupational territory, but the present affluence has made it easy for more of them to pursue a college education than ever before. The controversy today centers more on the type of education that is best for them than on the fact of it. Although women in other countries rarely go on to college unless they are preparing for a profession, such is not the case here, where 45 per cent of women high school graduates go to college. This is not to be deplored, for education is desirable and the pursuit of it is as fitting a way for a girl to spend her time before marriage as any other. Yet the style of learning offered should take into consideration the life plan of the average woman. Discussing female education in separatist terms is always inflammatory, for woman in her demand for equality lives in constant fear of derogation. It is hard for her to believe that a system of education designed especially for women could be *better*. If it is different from what men have, then in her mind it must be inferior. Nevertheless the average American woman is going to use her education in a different way from her male counterpart and is going to be available for educating at different times in her life. Her college experience should be attuned to this difference.

36

Although the average age at marriage in this country is dropping, the typical female high school graduate is not ready to take a husband and set up housekeeping, nor is she inclined to go to work immediately. A college campus provides an ideal environment in which to spend the interim period between high school and marriage. Here there is ample opportunity to meet new kinds of people and to try out various areas of intellectual and social experience. Coeducational colleges provide ample dating opportunities within easy reach, enhancing the possibilities of finding a compatible mate. However, if she is locked into a four-year curriculum, a girl often feels reluctant to break off her education by marrying even though she may be psychologically and emotionally ready to do so. Pressure is usually put upon her by family and faculty to take advantage of her only opportunity for education and remain in college until graduation. Once she is married, they insist, she will be far too busy being a homemaker and mother to continue her studies. Later on, after her children have left home, they argue, she will find herself without a degree and unable to engage in a satisfying occupation. Her years in college will have been wasted and she will be unhappy and frustrated—a victim of what Betty Friedan has termed the "disease without a name."

The average American woman is psychologically ready for marriage at the age of twenty and is most commonly married to a man about two years her senior, which would seem to mean that most girls should marry, as sophomores, men who are seniors and graduating from college. In our present educational system this would mean a termination of education for women in the middle of the college career. A few colleges

37

have adapted themselves to this psychological fact of life by a system of continuing education for women that would seem at least theoretically to provide an excellent answer. Residence is not required for earning a degree; instead, matriculation can continue after marriage by means of correspondence courses, part-time summer study, or credit obtained through attendance at extension or adult education courses at schools near their homes. In addition, refresher courses are offered for women beyond the child-rearing years to prepare these ex-mothers for interesting careers during the twenty or more years remaining when their children no longer demand their time and their husbands are most deeply absorbed in their own occupations.

It seems to be well established that girls of college age are not interested in studying home economics, interior decorating, or child psychology—sensible and useful as such courses would seem to be. College women consider themselves above such mundane matters and prefer to learn about them by experience later on. Therefore it is probably best not to vary the subject matter of the curriculum offered to women within a college, but only to tailor the degree requirements to their special needs.

A small proportion of women wish to pursue careers in science or the professions as primary interests, placing wifely or maternal duties in a secondary position or excluding them altogether. A recent survey has shown that this category is decreasing. While in 1930, 40 per cent of master's degrees were given to women, in 1963 only 31 per cent went to women, and the number of doctorates awarded slipped from 15 per cent in 1930 to only 11 per cent in 1963. Two and one-half per cent of our lawyers, 6 per cent of our doctors, 2 per cent of our senators, and .007 per cent of our federal judges are women. Most of these are doing well at their work and undoubtedly are happy doing it; but this is no reason to structure the education of women in general on the assumption that they will all pursue careers. Instead, female education ought to fit the life plan of the vast majority, who will benefit by concentrated education until marriage and then be able to devote only a limited amount of time to this purpose during the child-rearing hiatus, following which a resumption of intensive specialized training might be necessary before assuming the responsibilities of a career for later life. Some colleges, such as Goddard and Radcliffe, are starting to provide a continuing education program, and preliminary results are most encouraging.

Traditional institutions are slow to adapt themselves to social change, but success in the experiments now in process in the area of degree requirements for women and their continuing education should give encouragement to all those who want to plan women's education around the praiseworthy difference which exists between the psychological needs of women and those of men. These needs include a wish to satisfy basic maternal and "nest-building" instincts as well as intellectual ones. The life pattern of the average woman as well as her uniquely feminine personality deserve consideration in the planning of her education.

NEED FOR EXPANSION IN THE PRESTIGE COLLEGES

Coeducation itself was slow to catch on, but now is almost universally accepted as preferable. Formerly male bastions such as Hamilton are expanding to include women, and tradi-

39

tional women's colleges such as Smith and Mount Holyoke
have undertaken the sponsorship of a coeducational college.
This kind of expansion would seem to fill a serious need in
higher education. Despite the tremendous increase in the
number of college applicants, the established small universities
have not increased their enrollment to meet this new demand.
Claiming that larger size would lead to inferior quality of
education (a claim so far unproved), these prestige colleges
have consistently rejected as many as five or six applicants for
every one accepted. This has perhaps contributed as much as
any other one factor to the increased pressure on high school
students who, because of family tradition or desire for up-
ward mobility, are expected to compete fiercely in this con-
test in which the odds are strongly stacked against them. If
there is something advantageous about the size of the present
small colleges and universities, then affiliation with or sponsorship of junior as well as four-year colleges should be possible.
The advantages of this sort of "farm system" will be many. A
"junior" Yale or Princeton could serve as a testing ground for
students and faculty. Those who showed promise there could
move up to the main university, and those who found the
going too hard in the major institution could move down
either temporarily or permanently to the minor one. The facilities and the prestigious name of the sponsoring college
should give to its subsidiary campuses advantages which a
new college could not achieve for itself for decades.

Another way in which the most popular and traditional
colleges can meet the demands made by the army of applicants is to at least experiment with a full year semester system.
In the summer many huge dormitories, classrooms, and lab-

oratories lie idle while students and faculty enjoy vacation. By a simple readjustment of the term system these facilities could be utilized year-round and a considerably greater number of students could be enrolled without increasing the number in residence at any one time. Such a change would mean adding to the faculty, but with increased tuition income and the present availability of qualified teachers this should not pose a serious problem.

Now that America has committed itself to offering high level education to virtually everyone, it is time to find ways to adapt this education to the psychological make-up of the students to whom it is being offered. Educators tend to use criteria in their curriculum planning which are applicable to educators, teachers, and scholars. This is understandable but not rational. They must take into consideration the important fact that by temperament students are different. Some are at ease with abstract ideas and enjoy theoretical thinking. Others are concrete and practical in their approach to the world around them. They can analyze a motor or a complex political problem, but are left puzzled and confused when asked to analyze a piece of poetry or stream-of-consciousness prose. Still others can be excited only by a manual problem; they can take apart and construct delicate machinery or reproduce in pen and ink the minutest and most intricate design, but have no ability in reading or writing and no interest in it.

The mechanic and the analyzer should not be second-class citizens, educationally speaking. Their contributions can be as important in our world as those of the sophisticated scholar, and their talents can be sharpened and expanded by training and experience provided by an appropriate school or college.

Too frequently today the vocational school, the art school, the engineering or agricultural institute is derogated by teachers and administrators. Their prestige should be upgraded. Also, requirements which cannot be met by students who are limited in ability in one small area but brilliant in others should be relaxed and easily waived for those for whom they are difficult or impossible. To withhold a degree from a man inhibited in learning languages but capable in all other areas is no more logical than to deny a blind man one because he cannot pass an art appreciation course. Every student in college should be able to develop his particular talent to the fullest, unfettered by the need to fulfill requirements outside his interest and ability.

CHAPTER 3

Sex

Education is understood to be the responsibility of parents and the schools, and the role of each is fairly clearly defined. However, when it comes to giving knowledge and imparting standards of behavior in regard to sex, there is widespread confusion, not only about who should give the instruction but also about what should be said to young people on such important subjects as premarital intercourse, masturbation, and homosexuality. Attitudes toward these subjects are different now from what they were when the present generation of parents were adolescents. Such matters are talked about more freely, and much of the rationale behind the sexual mores of the thirties simply does not apply today. For this and many other reasons the patterns of sexual behavior are changing. The facts indicate that young people today are living by a different set of values in regard to sex than the generation preceding them.

The information which supports these conclusions lies in two principal areas: the figures for illegitimate births, and polls taken over the years which give us information about the number of women who have experienced intercourse before marriage. The national illegitimacy rate has more than tripled over the past twenty-five years. At the present time one out of every eighteen babies is born out of wedlock.

The first study related to premarital intercourse was done in 1929. It reported that 35 per cent of the women polled who were college graduates were not virgins at the time of marriage, as compared with 50 per cent of the college-educated men. By 1938 the figures had risen a little to 37 per cent non-virgins among women college graduates and 61 per cent of the men. This would seem to indicate that college men in the thirties were finding their sexual partners elsewhere than on their own campus. In 1953, two major polls taken by responsible teams of sociologists showed that the number of non-virgin college women graduates had risen to 50 per cent and of men to 67 per cent. It is important to realize that the statistics quoted apply to college graduates and do not provide any accurate estimate of how many of these women were or were not virgins at the time of graduation from college. Those who experienced premarital intercourse may have had their first experience before, during, or after college, but a number of college physicians and psychiatrists have stated that they believe the trend suggested by these surveys has continued during the ten years since the last published surveys. Statistics as well as professional opinion support the conclusion that more college men have intercourse with the girls they date instead of with prostitutes or pick-ups as in previous years. The custom of visiting the local whorehouse a couple of times a month while at the same time going steady with a nice girl seems to be less and less common. In addition, the "madonna-prostitute complex" which prevents young men from marrying because they can think of sex only in terms of a socially unacceptable type of girl whom they would not marry is reported to be less prevalent as a symptom in psychiatrists' offices. There are still many young men who paradoxically wish to find that the girl they marry is a virgin, but also expect to sleep with every girl they date before committing themselves to the one girl whom they expect by some magic to have remained pure. This is not a strictly modern masculine expectation. Witness William Shakespeare speaking through Ophelia (*Hamlet*, Act IV):

> Young men will do't if they come to't. . . .
> Quoth she, "Before you tumbled me,
> You promised me to wed."
> He answers:
> "So would I ha' done, by yonder sun,
> An thou hadst not come to my bed."

CAUSES OF THE CHANGE IN SEX MORES

This apparent trend toward greater sexual freedom in high school and college students may well be leading us toward a cultural morality close to what is now an accepted way of life in Norway and Sweden, where premarital intercourse has gained far greater general acceptance than here. The change is undoubtedly influenced, as it has been in Scandinavia, by the increasingly strong demand from women for equality on all levels. Apparently they have come to envy man's relatively greater freedom in the sexual area as much as they envy his wider vocational choices and higher salaries. Women perceive the double standard as keeping them from enjoying the pleasures of love-making which men enjoy without as serious social condemnation. This is not the universal feminine attitude, but there is a significant female rebellion against traditional masculine sexual prerogatives—not in the direction of curbing men but rather toward releasing women.

Improvement in the efficiency of contraceptive techniques by the discovery of oral contraceptives, and the spreading of information about them in magazines and the press, have contributed to lessening the fear of unwanted pregnancy. Physicians feel quite free to fit diaphragms without asking whether the request comes from a married or unmarried individual, and drugstores are less and less particular about requiring a prescription when they sell contraceptive pills, as evidence accumulates about their relative safety and lack of toxicity. Girls speak quite unashamedly with each other about contraceptive methods.

Despite the widespread knowledge of contraceptive techniques and the ease and simplicity with which they can be employed, a number of young people simply do not listen or prefer to ignore what they hear. Many of the girls who become pregnant claim never to have been told how to prevent conception. Others have been misinformed. If we face the facts—for example, that there were 201,700 reported illegitimate births in 1957, and that 10 per cent of all the women in the country have had a premarital pregnancy—then we cannot avoid the conclusion that we must more seriously assume the responsibility of informing our daughters, accurately and completely, about how to protect themselves and particularly their innocent offspring from the tragedy and injustice of illegitimacy. Those who argue that talking about birth control encourages licentiousness are not facing the facts about where we stand at the moment and where we are going. Information of this sort should be part of the curriculum in late high school and college. It can be taught in the context of giving helpful advice—not in a moralizing fashion, nor with the assumption that every listener will be using contraceptives before marriage.

Another factor partly responsible for the increase in premarital sexual relations is a decline in the impact and effectiveness of church training and religious experience. The modern emphasis on science, with its factual, strictly rational, and unemotional approach to issues of all kinds, has contributed to a rejection on the part of some young people of traditional ethical principles which are based on religious precepts and an essentially spiritual sense of good and evil. Adolescents today more than in earlier times are demanding logical reasons for ethical standards. It does not suffice to speak to them in terms of some kind of natural moral law or a *feeling* of what is right and wrong. They need also to know that the consequences of their behavior are going to be harmful, or disadvantageous to their own success or happiness, to be willing to restrain themselves and to exert self-control. Feelings of guilt or fear of eternal damnation simply do not have the inhibiting and

47

restricting effect on adolescents which they did a generation ago. There are still many young men and women for whom absolute morality has meaning, and their high standards need to be reinforced by their religion as it is presented to them by their priests, ministers, and rabbis within church and temple as well as in counseling encounters.

Kinsey, reporting in 1953, found that religiously devout women were about 20 per cent more likely to be virgins at the time of their marriage than those he described as "inactive" in regard to religion. This proportion remained the same irrespective of denomination, being nearly equal in women of Protestant, Catholic, and Jewish faith. Religious tradition is the slowest of all traditions to yield or bend to new discoveries and it can hardly be used as an accurate guide to what is psychologically best for all in terms of moral behavior. Still, to those for whom the old standards are most comfortable, for whatever reasons, religion can be an important bulwark. The tendency of some religious counselors to abandon a spiritual appeal in favor of a more down-to-earth psychiatric one appears to have lost them some formerly devout followers, and this hybrid approach has attracted very few. It would appear that through the present transition period a thoroughgoing traditionally religious approach should be maintained by church leaders and advisers for the benefit of those who can be truly helped by this kind of guidance and this kind only.

Progress toward a way of life that will allow sexual intercourse without legal or ethical restrictions for those who are unmarried appears to some observers to be healthy progress and not to represent a lowering of moral standards or in any sense a degeneration of our culture. Rather it is seen as a *change* in the ways men and women are to be allowed to behave sexually with each other. There are two aspects, however, in which such a change should be seen as the beginning of a generally harmful rather than a healthy trend. These are, first, in regard to illegitimacy, and second, in the effect of such a change upon the institution of marriage itself.

CAUSES OF UNWANTED PREGNANCY

The figures cited above show that illegitimate births are on the rise—despite the increased efficiency and dissemination of birth control information. The continued rise in unwanted pregnancies is directly related to the increase in premarital and extramarital intercourse, which in turn is often a function of the unconscious desire of one or the other partner to get or make pregnant. For some girls neither the enjoyment of intercourse nor the achievement of orgasm is sufficient proof of femininity. Although consciously they may believe they have no desire to have a baby, unconsciously they may harbor a strong wish to prove themselves adequate as women by producing a child. This unconscious need for fulfillment is often manifested by a refusal to use contraception or by "forgetfulness" in this regard. In some girls it is expressed by transparent rationalizations such as "It takes away the feeling" or "If you really love me you will take a chance." For still other girls, becoming pregnant constitutes a means of binding a man more closely. It increases his obligation and may force him into marriage.

Girls coming to college from high school, particularly

those who live far from the campus, are bound to feel lost and lonely during their first months away from home. They are particularly open to the development of overly dependent, desperate relationships. A graduate student told a typical story of this sort to a marriage counselor a few years ago. She had come to college at sixteen from a small town in Iowa. An only child of deeply religious parents, she had been carefully brought up but had always been adventurous—eager to be independent and to explore new horizons. Coming to college seemed to her second only to entering heaven itself. During the early weeks of her freshman year, she thought she was very happy but spent much of her time writing home about how happy she was—usually a good indication of underlying loneliness. At a get-together dance she met a senior who seemed to her exceptionally mature. He had been brought up locally and knew his way around town. The relationship burgeoned into a highly emotional love affair. The two were inseparable and the sexual attraction on the man's part was very strong. The girl's whole life centered on him, and rather than risk losing her principal emotional prop she began sleeping with him in his college room. Sex relations were not pleasant for her, because of the strong guilt she felt and because she believed she was not satisfying him. Unconsciously she began to fear he would leave her. Several times she lied to him about her "safe" period, and before long she was pregnant. After much soul searching the couple were secretly married. She left college for a year, then returned to finish her studies while her husband worked at the family shoe store. He became more and more mundane and boring to her. She wanted to study medicine and had broad intellectual and political interests, while he was interested only in merchandising and watching television. Neither of them could muster much interest in their baby. In the end they were divorced. She went on to medical school and he stayed with the store. Neither has remarried and the baby is being brought up by grandparents.

Young men also may feel an unconscious need to prove their virility by impregnating a woman. Good performance as a lover, even with a number of different girls, often does not make them feel truly manly until they know that their efforts have proved fruitful. Sometimes sophisticated unmarried couples who come for help after the girl is pregnant claim to be utterly mystified as to how they could have been so careless as to allow pregnancy to occur. Investigation reveals in many such instances that the young man involved has had feelings of inferiority and fears of inadequacy. He may have had a need to prove himself, and his neglect of protective measures on numerous occasions often is clearly related to times when he felt particularly ineffective and was more than usually moved to demonstrate his potency.

RESULTS OF UNPLANNED PREGNANCIES

The steps necessarily taken following an unplanned pregnancy—adoption of the child, abortion, or premature marriage—are clearly unfortunate ones, and their increasing frequency would seem to be a cogent argument for holding the line against permissiveness on the part of parents and college authorities toward premarital intercourse.

Another factor to be considered is the effect of unlimited experience before marriage on postmarital sexual behavior. Kinsey found that 29 per cent of the married women in his sample who were not virgins when they were married had at least one affair after marriage by the age of forty, whereas only 13 per cent of those who were virgins at marriage had become involved in an extramarital sexual relationship by the same age. These statistics cannot be interpreted as proving that premarital intercourse causes extramarital affairs, for it could be logically assumed that women who give up their virginity early are characterologically more inclined to be liberal in their attitude toward sex. They might well be inclined toward a postmarital affair by nature, and their earlier sexual activity cannot be construed definitely as a causative factor in their later behavior. However, the correlation between premarital intercourse and postmarital affairs at least suggests that one influences the other. While it is true that affairs are more readily tolerated today by both husbands and wives, still infidelity by one or another partner constitutes grounds for divorce in many instances. Anything that contributes to the shockingly high divorce rate in this country and the consequent ill effects upon children should be discouraged, and encouragement of premarital sexual relations would seem to be contributory.

In Scandinavia, attitudes toward premarital sex are far more liberal than in this country and sociologists have made careful studies of the effect upon marriage of this more permissive morality. They have found that since the stigma of marrying a girl who is already pregnant has been removed, the incidence of divorce has not risen but the number of extramarital affairs has increased. It would seem logical to assume that a family environment which includes a philandering father or a promiscuous mother or both would be less healthy for children than one in which fidelity prevailed. Another observation made by students of the Scandinavian "utopia" is that since the advent of the new morality there has been an increase in the number of orphans put up for adoption. Reluctance on the part of engaged couples to go through with marriage after pregnancy has occurred seems to account for this significant increase in illegitimate births. The Scandinavian experiment, then, does not provide us with convincing evidence that acceptance of the sex act as part of courtship contributes anything helpful to the climate of the marriage and the home after the wedding—if the latter indeed takes place at all.

ATTITUDES OF PARENTS AND SCHOOLS

Parents as well as authorities in schools and colleges should not be ahead of the times in their attitudes toward sexual morality. Instances of pushing children and students too far and too fast in this respect are common. Most psychiatrists are familiar with fathers who arrange liaisons for their sons with prostitutes or other women of easy virtue in order to "make men" of them. There are mothers, too, who slip a diaphragm to daughters who had no thought of becoming sexually involved until that very moment. Colleges often unwittingly condone or encourage sexual behavior in their students which is far in advance of the cultural and family mores of the moment. Men's colleges, for instance, in response to the demand of students, as early as 1952 changed their rules to allow girls to be entertained in the dormitory rooms. Such permissiveness can have serious emotional consequences.

A sophomore at one of these colleges came to the psychiatric clinic in a deep depression precipitated by overwhelming fears about being a homosexual. The story he told, though more dramatic and extreme than most, was typical in character of many that are heard in college health clinics. He lived in a two-bedroom suite with a pair of classmates. Two afternoons a week one roommate had exclusive use of the rooms, and on three other afternoons the second roommate took over to make love with his girl of the moment. These young men were quite sure that they were entirely justified in asserting their right to use the rooms for these sexual forays. Though there would have been some encroachment on their activities by further sharing, they expressed both contempt and surprise that the third inhabitant of the rooms did not engage in similar pleasures. One day they taunted him until he agreed to be "fixed up," and a tryst was arranged by them for him with a girl, who was primed to exert her seductive charms to the fullest and lure him into a sexual experience. As might be expected, the student found himself impotent in this situation for which he was neither emotionally nor sexually ready. He brooded about his failure and became convinced that he was hopelessly perverted. His roommates eventually became concerned enough about his state of mind to take him to a psychiatrist. Treatment was successful in restoring this student to emotional health; but the problem would never have arisen had pressure from the environment not forced him into a situation for which he was unprepared.

When the authorities at these colleges liberalized their dormitory rules, they did not do so in expectation that the bedrooms would become love nests. The students requesting the changes were asking that they be trusted to behave in a circumspect fashion. Perhaps the leaders who persuaded the administrations to change their policy did intend only to share study dates and engage in intellectual discussions with their girls in the living rooms of the suites, but it seems ironic that a college dormitory should be the only place where unmarried couples can legally share a bedroom. No hotel, motel or club and few private homes would allow this. It is easy to register at a motel with a girl who is not one's wife, but this involves using a false name, making patently obvious the fact that a law is being broken. Many universities, including some respected women's colleges, have liberalized their dormitory regulations in recent years, perhaps unaware that they are giving tacit consent to the mutual enjoyment of the hospitality of a bed. This is a generosity above and beyond that given or approved of by most parents as well as by the law of the land. Such permissiveness seems to put an unhealthy degree of pressure on that segment of the student population looking for help in controlling their physical impulses, as well as on that other group of students who are not ready to meet this kind of challenge.

Some women's colleges have given up rules about signing in and allow their students unlimited overnight permissions. This has deprived some girls of a protection that had been valued highly. The number of students who need to be able to say that the college requires that they sleep in the dormitory may be smaller than the number who would like unlimited freedom in this regard, but this more dependent minority deserves support from college authorities.

After such a policy change in one college, a student contributed to the college newspaper a poem entitled "Cassandra, or Virtue Rewarded," that read in part:

The evening pressed on and so did he
But his argument weakened at a rapid rate
For the later it got the more she was right
In saying "It's liable to keep me too late."
So at half past twelve she rose to go
And he said, "Cassandra, you may think it's fun."
She repulsed him secure in her purity and
The thought she had to be in by one.

So she went to her virginal pillow in peace
And awoke next morning to find by her side
A note to a bunch of white roses attached
Saying, "Cassie my dear, will you please be my bride?
For a man must take pleasure wherever he can
But in choosing the mother of his son
He wants a woman faithful and strong
And bound and determined to be in by one."

Generally speaking, the late adolescent is not psychologically mature enough for adult sexuality. The average college undergraduate, by nature, prefers an emotional and a physical relationship with the opposite sex which is intimate and private but not one which includes intercourse. Dr. Paul Walters, a Harvard Health Service psychiatrist, in his excellent paper "Promiscuity in Adolescence" observes, "The sexual impulse of the adolescent seems to be . . . diffuse and unfocused and consisting of vague longings for fusion with the loved object." By this he means an emotional fusion or identification rather than a physical one. Later in the same paper he states, "Premature sexual intercourse represents a serious failure in the development of the adolescent ego."

This is not to say that *some* students of college age are not mature enough to be comfortable in an adult sexual relationship (successful undergraduate marriages are proof of this) but it does point up that it is incorrect to assume that college students in general are asking for permission and facilities for enjoying sexual intercourse. In coeducational colleges that have given their students free access to bedrooms, the students themselves have asked that restrictions be imposed. They have sensed a pressure to engage in a type of sexual activity which felt inappropriate to them.

AREAS OF SEXUAL PERPLEXITY FOR COLLEGE WOMEN

Further indication that college girls are confused and distressed about the rapidity with which sexual mores are changing can be gleaned from the nature of the questions they ask in courses on marriage and dating given under the auspices of university health or counseling services. Such lectures, with opportunities for girls to hand in written questions, have been held at several girls' colleges recently. Typical questions, framed a little differently in the various colleges but similar in general nature, are:

1. What are the psychological and physical effects on boys of heavy petting?

2. How can a boy be brought to orgasm short of intercourse?

3. Is it true that premarital intercourse prepares a girl for greater sexual happiness in marriage?

4. Do individuals want sex more after once having experienced intercourse?

5. Does petting to climax become a habit and something which becomes more desired than intercourse?

6. Name the reasons why a girl should be a virgin at the time of marriage.

Reading between the lines of these questions and judging from the reactions of the girls to answers frankly given, it seems clear that the problem of how to justify virginity against the importunate demands of the men whom they love is uppermost in the girls' minds. Because society today still derogates the non-virginal woman more than the sexually experienced young man, these girls feel an understandable reluctance and a hesitation about being able to take their places happily and guiltlessly as complete sexual partners to their boy friends before marriage. College rules and expressed parental attitudes should bolster and protect both the girls and the young men who are not yet ready to adopt for themselves the standards of what appears to be a movement toward greater sexual freedom. Those ready to take their place in the vanguard will find ways to live by their own rules. Colleges should be careful not to push their students ahead of what is normal by present-day cultural and family standards, but instead should take a clear and firm stand in the middle of the continuum. Their responsibility *in loco parentis* and their humanitarian feeling for their students leave them no other choice.

CONFLICT OF VALUES BETWEEN HOME AND SCHOOL

While colleges should not by their regulations or lack of them imply a moral attitude which is more liberal than that of the average family or our culture in general, parents must not be too old-fashioned in imposing restrictions which in turn reflect a code of ethics to be complied with or rebelled against by their children. When parental standards which have become internalized and made part of conscience come too drastically in conflict with the standards of a college community, serious illness can develop.

A few years ago, a college freshman sought psychiatric help on the recommendation of her college adviser because of a fear of being with people which was so severe that she had been unable to leave her room for two weeks. In the course of her treatment it became clear that this regression was directly related to the girl's conflict over sex. She had been brought up in a highly moral family, one in which great emphasis had been placed on religion. After attending parochial schools she had been sent to a church boarding school for girls. Her father, who was a lawyer, forbade her dating during high school years but seemed little concerned about her choice of college—feeling, apparently, that she would have learned sufficient self-discipline and been indoctrinated solidly enough with high moral standards to remain for the rest of her life uninfluenced by contemporaries or by lax authorities. His daughter chose a rather unorthodox college where the curriculum emphasized music and the arts rather than the more usual course material. It was located near a larger men's college, and a free and easy attitude had been adopted by both institutions with regard to visiting privileges.

While this girl knew what she was getting into, and had purposely picked a college that would allow her to "live a little," she was surprised to find no limits set upon behavior by the institution or by the student government. Within a few days she had consciously decided to have an affair, feeling completely reconciled in her mind to the good sense of her decision and experiencing no conscious fear or uncertainty about it. It was not long before she found a sophomore in the "brother" college who was attractive to her and was glad to cooperate in this project to broaden her experience. Only two days after starting her affair, she began to feel nervous in class. Within a week her symptoms had increased to the point where she could not go to the dining hall and had to have her meals brought to her by her roommate. During the following two weeks, before her condition was reported to her faculty adviser, she felt too frightened to leave her room at all, and became so anxious when girls other than her roommate came to her room that she would vomit. Not until she had been in treatment for several months was she able to believe that her symptoms were related in any way to her sexual experience. For weeks she maintained that, in her mind, having an affair was perfectly moral and something she had wanted to undertake for a year or two before she came to college. She was sure that she had experienced no qualms about having intercourse and had thoroughly enjoyed it. Gradually, as she became acquainted with her unconscious, she began to feel the guilt she had been repressing and to understand that it was her shame which had made her avoid her colleagues and hide in her room.

BASIS FOR MORALITY TODAY

This girl's case is a good example of how logic can be undermined by feeling. Yet this story will not dissuade every logically minded young person who is arguing the good sense of premarital intercourse. What, then, can be used as a basis for morality, now that fear seems to have lost its effect for so many? Formerly fear of venereal disease, fear of pregnancy, and fear of hell-fire had meaning enough to be emotionally effective in maintaining the old standards of chastity and continence. If these standards lead to a more stable way of life for society as a whole, and there is good evidence that they do, then by what means can they be made meaningful to today's college and high school students? Undoubtedly, by dealing with them on their own terms and in their own language, *quid pro quo* logic, in addition to reinforcing the previously effective bases for those who are helped by them.

One premise, which it is logical to assume but over which there is bound to be controversy, is that the double standard has some merit and is backed up by certain clearly definable differences between men and women that go beyond the anatomical. The three relevant ways in which these differences are manifested are principally in the distinctiveness of female jealousy, sexual arousal, and orgasm. While some may argue that the influence of our culture (specifically the male attitude) may have brought about the presently characteristic feminine reactions in these three areas, such a stand is hard to defend, since these attributes appear to be deeply and basically set within the personality.

Women feel strong jealousy. "Hell hath no fury like a woman scorned" is proved an eternal verity many times each day, and the quality of this jealousy seems to be distinct from that of the male. A girl resents with bitter hatred a current intrusion upon the relationship between herself and her lover, but past liaisons cause her far less concern. Men, on the other hand, because of the high premium they put on their own degree of virility as it compares with others, feel jealous of all competition present or past. The fact that so much importance is attached to virginity by fiancés and so little by fiancées is only one example of this difference in the character of jealousy in the two sexes. Others can be seen in the relative indifference girls show about the previous dating experience of their boy friends, as opposed to the paranoid rage so frequently displayed by men who have found out or think they have found out about sexual dalliance on the part of their wives or girl friends. Women become exceedingly and perhaps as unreasonably angry at other women who steal their husbands' affections, but purely sexual adventures do not inspire such consuming rage. Women do not feel as basically threatened by competition in the sexual realm as do men.

Sexual appetite without specific physical arousal is not naturally as strong in women as in men. Most women do not feel hungry for a sexual experience until they have become accustomed to it or are excited by a kiss or other form of physical contact. The fact that fewer girls masturbate than men would seem to be a result of their relatively less powerful feeling of frustration. Men think about sex more than women, and their urges are subject to a stronger and more frequent ebb and flow. Most girls, if not involved in necking and petting situations, could postpone intercourse until after marriage without any feeling of deprivation, whereas most men could not.

Female orgasm is more difficult to achieve, comes later in the sexual act, and is usually possible only in the context of love and trust. It is more prolonged and gentle in nature than that of the male. These facts seem to reinforce the general impression that sex has a different meaning to a woman than to a man in both physiological and psychological terms, and leads to the logical conclusion that there should indeed be separate standards for each sex. However, a return to the old practice which allowed men a moderate degree of sexual freedom while women were expected to remain chaste would bring back the days of the brothel, the harlot, and the back street wife—with all the vice and crime involved.

If we follow "old-fashioned" logic we end up with a restoration of the double standard and its many disadvantages; if we follow the present generation's logic we may increase illegitimacy and weaken the marriage and family bond. There seems to be no thoroughly satisfactory answer to the problems presented by our instinctual sex drive. Perhaps this is why the story of the eating of the apple in the Garden of Eden is so deeply appealing. The serpent brought about the release of a force within man and woman which is beyond our complete comprehension and control; yet without it we would not exist at all. In the end we probably must be content to watch the pendulum swing from permissiveness to restrictiveness and back again, as each generation becomes dissatisfied with what it has inherited from the previous one and strives to find another answer to a problem as old as mankind itself.

This perplexing situation needs to be defined in honest terms to high school and college students. Parents are usually too embarrassed and unsure to provide the necessary facts, or to discuss frankly the basic ethical and practical issues with their adolescent sons and daughters. Often they can deal with the straightforward anatomical questions of young children, but they add to the confusion as well as increase the shame and guilt of their teen-age children by trying to do what is far better handled by discussion groups in schools, colleges, and churches.

CHAPTER 4

Drugs

Any discussion of the use of drugs by college and high school students must make clear in the beginning the distinction between the medical and the moral aspects of the subject. The physical damage done to the human body through the ingestion of most drugs is minor except in instances of overdosage or individual allergic reaction. Notable exceptions to this rule of course are cigarettes. Although the actual drug in the inhaled smoke causing damage is not known, proof that physical damage occurs in the lungs is now conclusive.

Individuals are able to take some drugs consistently over a period of years without permanent detrimental effect upon their body or body functioning. Psychological effectiveness may, however, be markedly reduced, and this is the principal

65

cause for the strong prejudice against drug taking on the part of society as a whole. Stories and pictures of the opium dens in China have made us acutely aware of the degenerating effects of allowing unrestricted distribution and use of narcotic drugs. One must remember this deleterious over-all effect of permissiveness when discussing the effects of each separate substance. Otherwise it is difficult to justify the extremely harsh penalties presently meted out for the possession or sale of some drugs which in themselves seem relatively harmless and even beneficial.

Strictly from a medical standpoint, reliance on a morning dosage of Benzedrine for energy and optimism during the day cannot be termed unhealthy. As long as the amount taken is not escalated to a toxic level and the individual is not sensitive to the drug, no harm will be done. On the other hand, such a dependence upon an artificial source of good humor seems immoral—even though two martinis in the evening for the same purpose are considered appropriate and proper by a large part of our population.

The daily use of insulin or cortisone to maintain normal body function is not condemned, but similar use of Benzedrine, tranquilizers, or marijuana to maintain a desirable mood is legislated against or felt to be a sign of moral weakness. Although young people such as those who support the LEMAR (legalize marijuana) organization argue that there is an inconsistency here, the fallacy of their argument is clear. In too many cases dependence upon drugs leads to ineffectiveness and lack of productivity.

Many adults, particularly in Great Britain, argue that the problems which arise from drug addiction stem from the

66

desperate behavior of those who need and cannot obtain the drugs, not from the direct effect of the drugs themselves. This is in large part true, but allowing addicts to obtain drugs more freely would lead to far worse consequences in terms of increasing the addict population, eliminating many of these individuals from the ranks of the employable and the productive. While it appears to be true that there is a personality type susceptible to addiction and that the vast majority of the population would not become addicted even if they were given drugs experimentally, there are large numbers of potential addicts who will never become addicted because drugs are relatively unavailable to them.

Many wonder whether there is greater use of drugs by young people today than ten years ago. The answer probably depends more on fluctuations in supply than on any other factor, for demand has always exceeded supply. There is evidence, however, that drugs are now being used by a younger group, and that the greater amount of cash in the hands of teen-agers has made this group more attractive to pushers.

MOTIVES FOR DRUG TAKING

The reasons why drugs have so strong an appeal to the adolescent are several. The reason most commonly cited is rebellion, and this probably is a factor of importance in most instances.

Children begin at about fourteen to gain satisfaction from doing the opposite of what is expected. This is a way of retaliating against parents for years of what now is felt to have been unjustified subjugation. It is also an attempt to find a way of life and a personality which are individual, separate, and not superimposed by others. Anything that is disapproved of by adults begins to have a certain allure, whether in the realm of dress, hairdo, manners, study habits, or music appreciation. Drugs are clearly beyond the pale in the eyes of both parents and legal authorities, and thus have a particularly strong appeal. A lot of the mystique that is part of the drug taking experience is directly related to the satisfaction the participants gain from realizing how horrified their parents would be to know what was going on. The secrecy surrounding meetings, the colorful slang words, the underworld affiliations make it all seem very naughty. The taking of drugs to satisfy rebellious impulses is not usually a factor in cases of hard core addiction, but plays a part more often in the case of the experimenter who tries it once or twice and does not find it pleasurable enough to continue.

A much more frequent motive than rebellion for the consistent user of drugs is the search for a change in personality. An individual who feels inadequate or perhaps perverted sees in drugs a way out of himself and into a totally new body and mind. For some a drug does give temporary surcease from feelings of inferiority, but for most it provides only numbness and moderate relief from anxiety, with no true or constant feeling of strength or superiority. Often this search for a new self is what leads to escalation and a frantic search for new drugs that may lead on to addiction.

Adolescence is a time when acceptance from adults and the peer group is hardest to gain. Physical as well as emotional factors militate against the needed appreciation and affection. Clumsiness, acne, and temporary obesity are often present;

68

and in the emotional area uncertainty, apathy, or rapidly
shifting moods make the adolescent hard to like. He is often
overcome with self-disgust and hopelessness. At such times
the chance to become outgoing, uninhibited, or the life of the
party by "turning on" is exceedingly tempting. The possibility that he may not be able to "turn off" does not seem likely,
although to some it may even appear desirable.

Many adolescents are intrigued by death. Their poetry is
full of allusions to the grave and even some of their popular
songs are concerned with tragedy and early death. The reason
is obscure, but may well be tied up with a sense of time pass-
ing frighteningly fast which accompanies the rapid physical
and emotional changes that are occurring during this period
of development. It also may be related to a pervasive feeling
of alienation and estrangement experienced by many adolescents. This can lead to preoccupation with the total estrangement that comes with death and the distress it will
bring to those who now do not seem to care. This fascination
with dying may lead to a cavalier attitude toward danger and
a willingness to tempt fate in various ways such as playing
"chicken" in cars or "Russian roulette." Taking drugs may be
seen as attractively dangerous. The risk of addiction can make
drug experimentation appealing.

Still another compelling reason for taking drugs, particularly marijuana, is the sense of communication or togetherness
that can result. Individuals who feel isolated and self-conscious
seem to gain an ability to participate and to share a group
experience when in a drug-induced state of mind. Observers
not themselves under the influence of drugs have often expressed amazement at the results reported, for actually little

conversation takes place during such sessions, and individual members of the group look ill at ease and more separate from each other than under normal circumstances. Still, in retrospect the sessions are recalled by those who did smoke marijuana as relaxed and warm with a deeply rewarding nonverbal communication having taken place.

Treatment of the individual for whom drugs are appealing is often discouraging. The personality disturbance which leads to addiction is deep-rooted and hard to change. The reaching out for help in the form of an external thing rather than a person makes psychotherapy or counseling extremely difficult. This was demonstrated in the case of Dan, a boy of sixteen when he first was brought to a therapist by his father for help. His original problem centered on school work and was clearly more upsetting to the father than to the boy. Dan was failing all his courses in high school and seemed headed for the dropout pile. The father was the owner of a small business, a college graduate, and held high ambitions for his children. Dan's mother was a strong person with an artistic temperament. She was a talented sculptress who had been through art school and had exhibited at a number of shows. She was enthusiastic about Dan's work in sculpture at times, but usually seemed preoccupied with her own work and rather cold toward what others in the family were doing. Occasionally she would have temper tantrums in the course of which she would pick on Dan, accusing him of laziness and lack of consideration for others. There was an older brother, Ned, who had esoteric interests, had dropped out of two colleges, and was known to have smoked marijuana. He had traveled with a beatnik group with which he had felt quite at home—unlike Dan who aspired to friendship with the more aristocratic boys in the neighborhood.

Dan himself was flabby, big in the buttocks and hips, narrow-shouldered, had curly black hair and a somewhat childlike face. He was obviously intelligent, with an excellent vocabulary and an unusual capacity for abstract thinking particularly in regard to himself. He enjoyed introspection to a certain depth, and appeared able to evaluate himself in relation to the world around him realistically. Although he had a casual and falsely optimistic view of his academic future, he freely admitted that he was unhappy about his total life situation.

In the course of his early interviews Dan revealed that he had a predilection for drinking cough syrup by the bottle. He did this alone, and explained that he had heard that certain of these preparations contained substances that could make a person "feel different." Assurance that this was not true did not cure him of the habit. Shortly afterward he reported making friends with a teacher who was boiling down paregoric to extract the opium contained in it and injecting this into his vein. Dan professed to be both fascinated and horrified by this procedure, but promised he would never go along with it.

After a year of treatment and transfer to a nearby boarding school Dan was doing fairly well academically, but his dabbling with drugs was becoming more and more time consuming. He had begun taking Benzedrine daily, paying enormous sums to friends to keep him supplied, and was also dealing in marijuana. At this point the therapist tackled the drug problem head on by forbidding their use; but Dan claimed that above all else he wanted to prove himself sexually and felt he could not approach a girl or be potent in intercourse unless he was "changed psychologically" by some kind of drug. He felt unmasculine, passive, and ineffectual, because of his body build and what he believed to be a strong identification with his mother. He saw himself developing just as she had, and he conceived of this as a predestined course which could only be temporarily halted by some magical combination of drugs. Insights gained in psychotherapy seemed to make no dent on his behavior.

In the course of the next summer Dan was picked up on the Mexican border with a sack of marijuana in his spare tire. Complicated legal proceedings followed and he was finally released. He became somewhat of a hero in his neighborhood group as a result of this episode and showed no remorse, nor did he recall any true fear during the experience. Some sexual success followed this adventure, but soon Dan was again attempting to alter his personality by trying new drugs. This time he experimented for the first time with an intravenous heroin "fix." The fear which preceded the injection and the "all gone" sensation when he was under the influence made Dan swear he would never do it again.

It was not many months later, however, before he was "turned on" again, and at this point his therapist felt that he must take a firmer stand than previously. He discussed hospitalization with the boy, and implied that he could not take responsibility for further treatment if these incidents were repeated. This approach simply led to Dan's disappearing and, when he was reached through friends, a refusal to return to treatment. Follow-up information covering two years since termination indicated that Dan was working at a menial job and still sporadically making use of drugs of all kinds.

Not all cases turn out as grimly as this one. Many young people when offered the opportunity can find answers to their personality problems through psychotherapy and can give up reliance on drugs, or can be prevented from beginning to use that solution. No one knows why one adolescent chooses to try drugs as an answer to his feelings of inadequacy, whereas others may become depressed, fail in school work, or take up fast driving; but drug taking is more treacherous and more dangerous than the other escapes, and all possible measures should be taken to close off this avenue and to turn back those who have started along it.

NARCOTICS

In strictly medical parlance, a narcotic is any drug that causes a depression of central nervous system function; but in legal terms the definition includes only those drugs which are under international control because they are addictive and dangerous. Certain drugs such as caffeine and tobacco are addictive in that withdrawal of them cause symptoms (nausea, stomach cramps, tremor) but they are not considered dangerous and are not classified as narcotics. The best known of the narcotic drugs are morphine, heroin, Demerol, and cocaine. They are primarily depressants and pain relievers. Cocaine is also a local anesthetic. In addition they produce a sense of dreaminess and well-being known medically as euphoria, and it is this effect which makes them so fatally fascinating to those not in need of sleep, analgesia, or anesthesia. The drug-induced mood is the first goal, but after a certain time, the length of which varies from one individual to another, this goal changes from a search for pleasure to one of

73

escape from the excruciating agony of withdrawal symptoms. Then taking narcotics becomes not a matter of choice but of necessity.

Although addicts have been taken through the period of withdrawal symptoms in hospitals, most of them return to the drug—apparently drawn by the memory of the euphoric experience. Many studies have been done in an attempt to understand what it is that characterizes the addict. Some researchers feel it is related to a strong dependency upon a mother who fosters and encourages this dependency, but this does not tell us very much that is useful for prevention. For many, the discovery of narcotics and their effects can be the beginning of a literal ruination of their lives. Such a potentially devastating experience should not be made available to them. It can be prevented by strict drug control and early education about the dangers inherent in experimentation.

Marijuana

Although classified as a narcotic in most states, marijuana does not by technical definition fall into this category. Most researchers do not feel that it is an addictive drug; it does not cause withdrawal symptoms, nor does it cause any permanently harmful physiological effects. However, it is frequently the precursor to the taking of truly addictive drugs. Those who traffic in it often push other more dangerous substances. For these reasons law enforcement agencies treat those who dispense or possess it as stringently as those found trading in morphine or heroin.

Marijuana is made from the flower of the hemp plant and is

known also as hashish or pot. It can be effective when chewed or sniffed but is usually smoked in the form of cigarettes known colloquially as reefers. Although some scientific investigators assert that its effects are entirely psychological, this is hard to believe, for users are unanimous in their description of its effects. They ascribe to it a feeling of lightness, happiness, and camaraderie which is unique, and much more peaceful than results from alcohol. A feeling of sexual competence also may be present, but even though most pot smoking occurs in groups, only rarely does sexual activity take place in the course of a session. For the most part the smokers are quiet. Conversation, when it does occur, concerns the sensations that each is undergoing as the drug takes effect.

Most college students who smoke marijuana do so as an experiment, and even though they claim the experience to have been pleasurable do not repeat it more than four or five times. There is always the danger, however, that this drug experience will be the beginning of long and varied attempts to resolve basic personality problems by the drug method. The most innocent of experiments can turn into a permanently damaging experience if it leads to arrest for a federal offense. University officials and parents must be on the alert to protect from such consequences those for whom they are responsible. Strict control of drug sources and pushers, as well as educational campaigns and disciplinary action against offenders, is helpful; but important also are facilities that provide counseling and psychological help to students in emotional trouble. Opportunities for challenge and healthy rebellion (as discussed later) are valuable as substitutes for drug experimentation.

PSYCHEDELIC DRUGS

Within the past several years a new group of drugs has become available to that segment of our youth looking for artificially induced changes in sensation and perception. These substances were originally used in strictly controlled scientific explorations into the nature of serious mental illness, and were administered to create states of mind in normal subjects which resemble schizophrenia. These drugs were originally called psychomimetic because of their ability to mimic psychotic illness in persons who were not ill. It was hoped that through experiments with these drugs a greater understanding of the chemical mechanisms operating in mental illness could be achieved. The results have been disappointing so far, and the experimental drugs (LSD 25 and psilocybin) have unfortunately since been used by pseudo-scientific workers for what they have termed psychedelic or consciousness expanding purposes. Under the guise of bringing about increased creativity and greater feelings of harmony and loving kindness, many students have been given these drugs—with tragic results in some cases. LSD and psilocybin have a physiologic effect which causes hallucinations, euphoria, and a sense of closeness in some individuals, and in others depression, panic, and suicidal or homicidal impulses. In some cases, these effects do not wear off in the usual six to eight hour interval following ingestion but may last for months or even a year. Some individuals have experienced recurring episodes of psychosis following a single dose of one of these psychedelic drugs. At present there is no known method of predicting for whom such an experience will consist of one short episode, and for

76

whom it may mark the beginning of a lifetime struggle against a crippling and terrifying emotional illness. For this reason it is essential that these drugs be kept under strict control and not be made available except to responsible medical investigators.

MESCALINE

For many centuries American Indian tribes have used the buds or buttons from peyote cactus plants to induce visions as part of their religious rituals. These buttons have recently been made available to the public at large and can be obtained through the mail from various distributors in Texas and Mexico. The active ingredient in the buttons is mescaline, a substance similar to that found in the "magic" mushrooms used in similar religious rites in Mexico.

The thrills of mescaline ingestion have been described by Aldous Huxley in his book, *The Doors of Perception,* and the terrors of it have been well documented by William James. Although some investigators have reported debilitating depression and an alarming trancelike state from taking mescaline, most student experiences with this drug are disappointing rather than harmful. The increased awareness of color and the impression that one possesses an exciting new creative ability are transient, and not real in the sense of producing great works of art or literature. Most students who experiment with this bitter tasting drug, which is not as pleasant or reliable as marijuana, do so only once or twice; but there is always the danger of progressing from mescaline to other more dangerous substances, and its use should be strongly discouraged.

SEDATIVES, STIMULANTS, AND TRANQUILIZERS

Whether or not to prescribe Benzedrine or a similar drug regularly for depression, obesity, or to prevent drowsiness is largely a moral question, as is the routine prescription of tranquilizers or sedatives for continual equanimity or consistent deep sleep at night. Some individuals need their nightly Nembutal capsule as much as others need their evening cocktail. To other more self-reliant individuals both these habits may seem immoral. Doctors themselves disagree about the ethics of prescribing stimulants and sedatives in maintenance dosage, but they all agree that when the dosage of any of these preparations is escalated close to or beyond the point of toxicity or safety, then the situation is an unhealthy one and calls for intervention.

There are students who take stimulants such as the amphetamines (Benzedrine, Dexedrine, etc.) and barbiturates (Nembutal, Amytal, Luminal, etc.) for kicks rather than for any of the medically indicated purposes. In the case of barbiturates this can lead to a habit which is as difficult to interrupt as an addiction to narcotics. While constant use of the amphetamines rarely leads to such extreme dependence—except in the case of an amphetamine such as Dexamyl, which is a combination of Dexedrine and sodium amytal, a barbiturate—still there is a danger in the escalation of these drugs. An extreme excitement can result from overdosage or from a period of wakefulness extended beyond normal endurance. This excited state may bring about hallucinations and delusions of persecution. Fortunately the drugs in these categories are distributed through normal drug channels and control can be more easily maintained than with the illegal ones that come into the country by secret means, or the experimental ones that go to research laboratories or to individual experimenters. Yet these prescription drugs are not controlled in the way they can or should be. More careful enforcement of the rules is in order, particularly in the many communities where young persons can gain access to the drugs without prescription.

ALCOHOL

Irresponsible use of alcohol is not limited to the younger generation and for that reason among others it is a difficult topic for discussion. It is indeed a dangerous drug, for it releases inhibition and impairs judgment—a poor combination of effects. Nonetheless, we are forced to deal with it since our "great experiment" of the twenties failed in its original intent to eliminate it and proved instead that alchohol, like atomic power, is here to stay.

Much of the havoc resulting from youthful driving and riotous behavior has been attributed to alcohol, but it has probably caused no more death and destruction for the young than for older people. Perhaps it is the greater sense of loss felt for the person dying young, or perhaps it is an idea that alcohol has a different effect on an adolescent than on an adult, that has made us so quick to impose laws and regulations on teen-age drinking. This may be a reasonable approach; the younger a person is, the less certain is his judgment, and there is less good sense in reserve when a part is dissolved by alcohol. An adolescent's impulses are naturally stronger and carry him away in more violent fashion when his inhibitions are lessened.

The older generation must walk a narrow line between

79

excessive restriction, which leads to rebellious drunkenness, and encouragement at an age when control mechanisms are not well developed. Most adolescents who are allowed to learn their own tolerance and capacity in safe circumstances at an age when they feel ready to try out alcohol will soon learn how to use it safely.

Chronic alcoholism is rare in adolescence. Approximately 3 per cent of those who drink become alcoholics later on in life. Tragic as each case is, this percentage does not impress a teen-ager about the ultimate risk involved. A sensible example set by the older generation, and help in learning drinking habits which are in keeping with his own tolerance, are the best means of preventing the tragedies that come from premature use of alcohol.

In forming our attitudes and rules about drugs we are handicapped by being unable to predict which young person is merely using a drug experimentally or on a dare, and which one is headed for a lifetime of despair. In order to protect the few who fall into the latter group we must strive to cut down on the supply of illegal drugs and see that those sold on pre-scription are carefully regulated. In addition, we must look to the needs of the person who is seeking answers to his per-sonal problems in drugs and help him find these answers else-where—by giving him understanding ourselves or through the help of others trained to do this, or by helping him to feel excited and satisfied by more healthy and genuine challenges.

CHAPTER 5

Riotous Behavior

While relatively few high school and college students become involved with drugs, a greater proportion engage in rebellion or wild behavior—either self-initiated or as the result of following a crowd with whom they wish to gain acceptance. Is this rebellion necessary? The question repeats itself over and over again in discussions between psychiatrists, parents, and administrators. Nonconformist behavior on the part of adolescents is designed to perplex and irritate authority, and it is no wonder that part of the perplexity centers on whether or not this striking out against parents, school, and society is avoidable. Is this an inevitable part of growing up— an essential temporary stage in the development of maturity? Is it preventable by stricter discipline and greater firmness?

81

Or is it a symptom of a sick generation of young people led by hoodlums and incipient criminals? Or, finally, is it a Communist-inspired plot to spread internal dissension in the United States?

There is truth to a varying degree in the implications of each question. Rebellion of a sort is necessary for healthy personality development, but the nature of this rebellion can indeed be influenced and modified by the attitudes and actions of parents, school, and society. The natural rebelliousness of this age group can be distorted by a few particularly undisciplined and impetuous bad actors, and there is some indication that in a few instances groups inimical to this country have capitalized on the capacity of masses of college students to disrupt the workings of important institutions.

In order to counteract the destructive influence of rebellion both on society and upon the individual himself it is important to understand in detail the complicated psychological relationship between the late adolescent and authority. This understanding begins with a knowledge of the emotional nature of the college and high school student.

THE MEANING OF REBELLION

He is an individual just beginning to be allowed responsibility and the privilege of making independent decisions. He feels at one moment eager for freedom, and at another childishly helpless to make a decision or to act independently. The childish feelings he is ashamed of, and he often tries to hide them from himself and from the outside world by pretending they do not exist or by overcompensating in the opposite direction. This overcompensation is praised at an early age, when precociousness manifested by acting grown up or being unusually poised is considered an asset, but in the late adolescent it takes a less praiseworthy form. Fears of dependence may be covered up by exaggeratedly independent action such as extremes in dress or hairdo. Feelings of inadequacy may be overcompensated for by making earsplitting sounds with motorcycle engines or outboard motors. Fast driving, excessive drinking, and stories of sexual conquest disguise a sense of inferiority and continuing childishness. Impulsive decisions, the refusal of advice or help from parents (other than financial), and affiliation with extremist leaders all represent a desperate attempt to prove something that may be actually true but does not yet feel so—an ability to be self-sufficient and self-reliant.

Sometimes rebellion takes a passive rather than an aggressive form. Students grappling with their own conflicting feelings about individuality and adequacy may find themselves overcome by apathy and lethargy—unable to care about achievement or accomplishment in any form. Their declaration of independence is to declare everything pointless or useless, indicating by their lack of participation a contempt for all that is held to be worthwhile by the rest of the world. Such individuals are not the ringleaders in riotous behavior, but often their passivity can be turned into open rebellion by others who are expressing the same basic hostility in a different way. Also, the apathetic student often has a deep self-hatred which can be projected outward onto others if he is exposed to an emotional group bent on retaliation against some real or fancied injustice.

✓ Some forms of rebellion serve a constructive purpose. They help the developing adult feel more capable as an individual and show him that he can dare to be different. The young teen-ager feels tied down to family tradition. He begins to believe that all his behavior and his thoughts are dictated from above. This marionette quality of his life irks him and he begins to want to break free. One way is to challenge the reasonableness of the precepts used to manipulate him. Soon he finds that parents can outreason him in a verbal encounter and he resorts to action as a way to prove he is right. "I can exceed the speed limit and not hurt anybody or get arrested." "I can stay out until 3 A.M. and still do my homework and not get sick." "See, I can seduce a girl and she won't get pregnant." A certain amount of this kind of defiance does help to free the individual, and usually he soon learns through his own experience or that of close friends that limits on impulses are necessary. He then can begin to build his own set of limits and develop a value system which he feels is his own and therefore valid. If this testing out process does not occur, there is a danger that feelings of incompetence and resentment against the encroachment of others will keep these individuals less effective and productive than they would be if given opportunity for healthy rebellion.

Parents are fond of pointing to "model boys" in the community and asking why all young people can't be like these paragons of virtue. They also often point to themselves or to other adults as examples of people who have grown into upright citizens without ever having gone through a "bad period." There have been no known long-term studies done on the careers of a sample of valedictorians, Eagle Scouts, heads of student government, or class presidents which might indicate the virtue of being to all outward appearance a model citizen when young; but probably such a study would reveal either hidden instances of nonconformist behavior or else a rather pallid and constricted adult life.

Rebellion does help the developmental process and contributes to the eventual achievement of an identity. It also serves as a means of attracting attention, and this function should not be forgotten. Adolescence is an awkward and an unattractive stage. Those in the midst of it feel keenly unappreciated. Nonconformist behavior (drug taking, as one example) can bring a reaction from authority. Often at this age a reaction of any kind, whether positive or negative, punitive or rewarding, is a welcome response. It has been found that delinquent behavior is more common in families where discipline is either extremely punitive or extremely permissive. Parents who are definite and firm but not excessively threatening rarely find that their children have serious difficulties with the law. On the other hand, teen-agers who are too afraid of being physically injured at home rebel against legal or school authority rather than parental. So, too, young people whose extreme behavior is tolerated without a murmur at home find satisfaction in the reaction of policemen or truant officers. Parents find it hard to know when to respond to the unspoken wish of the adolescent for firm limit setting, and when to accede to his audible demands for more freedom and responsibility. It is a difficult assignment to play the role of liberator and jailer alternately but appropriately; yet this is the key to guiding the teen-ager successfully through the turbulent years.

UNCONSTRUCTIVE REBELLION

Rebellion becomes unconstructive when it is expressed in ways which are permanently self-defeating to the individual, such as serious underachievement in school (see Chapter 2), or when it results in property damage or physical injury to others. Such extreme behavior is usually preventable, but when the seeds of the trouble have been planted early, what springs from them is hard to deal with.

Much attention has been given to riots in the past decade— those that have occurred in colleges and in various resort areas. The violence and the destruction in these recent brawls have been greater than in the easily remembered past and this has contributed to the concern. Part of this may be attributable to the sheer force of numbers. Forty per cent of the population of this country are now under twenty years of age. When adolescents congregate nowadays, whether it be for a folk festival, a football game, or to watch a playground fist fight, they may suddenly be a mob instead of a group. The old saying that there is safety in numbers applies to mobs. Each member feels both safe and powerful. With characteristic adolescent bravado, such mobs first demonstrate that they have strength and then want to test it out. Soon they are looking for targets and antagonists. Appropriately handled, they will meet their match early and recognize—even be glad to find—that they are not invincible. Once convinced that they have matched their strength against a greater force, they will usually retreat gracefully.

Those experienced in riot work know that by keeping a group constantly on the move, rabble-rousing speeches are prevented. The demonstrators do not have a chance to feel united nor do they have a common goal. Authorities working to control the demonstration try to break up the moving mass into smaller groups, bringing about a reduced feeling of safety and strength through numbers. Identification of individuals by name is also helpful. Several ominous looking college demonstrations have been quieted by faculty members who walked through the crowd simply saying to students they recognized, "Hi, Bill Jones," "Hello there, Bob Smith." Losing anonymity is dramatically dampening to a spirit of rebellion and destructiveness.

The increase in numbers of young people is not the only reason for the apparent rise in the frequency of riotous outbreaks and in the destructiveness involved. There is a violent quality about the young rioters of today which did not characterize the youthful rebel of the thirties and forties. The college students of those days seemed more lighthearted, and their outbreaks were more like an overflow of high spirits than the expression of vengeful resentment which seems to underlie many of today's explosions. Pranks such as disrupting the plumbing system by flushing every toilet in ten dormitories at a given moment, or placing a sudsy detergent in the college rowing tank, have considerably more humor and imagination to them than sitting in a classroom building for a two-day period or trampling the university president's fence into kindling wood. The type of behavior displayed at the resort riots, with their wanton destruction of property, terrorizing of the population, and injury real or threatened to innocent bystanders, is something new. It indicates a boiling rage combined with a deep contempt for law and order as well as a search for excitement of the most brutal sort; it does not augur well for the future, unless a change takes place in the way authority deals with the young.

CAUSES OF RIOTS

Boredom and righteous indignation seem to be the ingredients that most often make for an explosive milieu. Prevention of these two conditions is not always possible, but even when one or both are present careful handling can forestall a serious outbreak. Most resort riots have occurred over holiday weekends, during vacations, or in the brief interim between the conclusion of summer jobs and the start of the school term. These are times when scheduled activities are at a minimum and a good deal of loose energy is accumulating. Some communities welcome the young and encourage them to congregate. If it is the merchants hoping to sell beer, gasoline, and other explosive mixtures who are involved in preparing for this congregation of young people, the chances that trouble will occur are far greater than if youth leaders, agency workers, and recreation directors are included in the planning. A total atmosphere of welcome will help to keep a feeling of rejection from becoming the focal point for righteous indignation. Planned activities in fairly widely separated areas and well publicized, sensible rules and regulations have helped a great deal in many popular vacation towns. Limiting drinking to specified spots such as beaches or certain parks, bans on extremes in dress in the formal parts of town, and the presence *from the start* of ample numbers of uniformed protectors of the peace also seem to have a limiting effect on behavior without eliminating enjoyment.

88

Riots have always been part of the burden imposed upon authorities in colleges by their students but recently these insurrections seem to have become more violent and more vindictive. It is hard to say whether this is because the civil rights movement has given to civil disobedience some degree of honor which it never had before or whether it is because the students have more justifiable causes for complaint. Clearly, there is an increasing number of students demonstrating their dissatisfaction in a destructive way. In a number of cases, administrative actions seem to have been responsible for the riots themselves or for increasing the extent and the degree of their violence. Students expect authority to react to their rebellion but to react in a strong and unflustered manner and not to cave in no matter how strong the provocation. Dr. Carl Binger tells a story which epitomizes this ambivalent student attitude. During a riot in Harvard Square in the early days of this century, an elderly Cantabrigian emerged from the subway on his way home from his office in Boston. Amazed at the furore he found in the Square he asked a disheveled student who was rushing by what was going on and was told in reply, "We are rioting, Sir."

In order to become matters of serious consequence, student riots need to have a climate, a cause, and a trigger. Causes are a dime a dozen on most university campuses, and triggers can emerge from the most apparently innocent of any of the events of a single day. Administration and faculty, then, must concentrate their efforts on keeping the climate as healthy as possible in order to prevent the college from becoming a breeding place for violence.

In a college community it is virtually impossible to prevent causes for righteous indignation from cropping up. No one is capable of predicting what small change in policy or other administrative action will suddenly flare into a *cause célèbre* as contrasted with an apparently similar one which will go unnoticed. In one college, the changing of the language on the diploma caused a riot while the elimination of maid service in the rooms and dining halls caused nary a ripple of protest. In general, however, prior warning of a change, explanation of the rationale behind it, some opportunity for discussion, and as long an interim as possible between the time the decision is announced and the time it takes effect are all helpful preventive measures. The latter allows for continued discussion and also means that some students will graduate without having been affected by the change. Most important, however, is the need to remain firm about the decision once it is made—unless some previously unknown and important factor comes to light in the course of discussion with the students.

While the trigger for a student revolt may be an administrative decision, the emotional climate of the student body makes a great difference in the type of reaction. An emotionally healthy campus can absorb change of almost any kind without a violent protest, while one which is already tense, dissatisfied, or resentful is quick to pick on the smallest incident as justification for a major demonstration. Large colleges and universities tend to fall easily into this latter category. The increasing number of college age individuals in the population has led to a rapid increase in enrollment in many of the state-controlled universities. In these large institutions, student population has outgrown the faculty. Classes are larger and more impersonal. Part of the teaching load is being carried by teaching assistants who are graduate students only a shade older in age and educational experience than the students they are teaching. Undergraduates are dissatisfied with classes, section meetings, and seminars conducted by these inexperienced teachers, who in addition may be so burdened by trying to fulfill their own advanced degree requirements that they are unable to devote much time to individual students for extra tutoring or special projects.

Not only has the quality and the amount of the teaching become diluted by this process of rapid expansion, but counseling services have not been able to meet the increasing demand brought about by the skyrocketing enrollment. Budget directors are often quicker to add administrative workers than to allot funds to psychological or psychiatric services; as a result, students find few trained professionals to whom they can turn for help when tensions build up. Instead they may be dealt with by administrators trained exclusively in personnel fields whose guiding slogan is "No trouble." Such individuals often deal peremptorily with disgruntled students and are uninterested in understanding the cause of the trouble, hoping instead that it will be ironed out by the wheels of a computer-like system designed to spot trouble and eliminate it without requiring people to become involved with people. Such automated, depersonalized ways of dealing with students have caused growing resentment in the undergraduate body of many colleges. The students feel rejected and cast aside. They are still at an age when they need a considerable degree of personal appreciation. Distinctness and singularity in the ways he is dealt with by others are important to the late adolescent. He is not yet ready to find these in relationships with a wife and children of his own, but he has passed the stage where he

YOUTH AND THE HAZARDS OF AFFLUENCE

he can gain them from the parents he is growing away from. He still feels a need (although he would not define it this way) for attention and understanding from parental substitutes.

The housing facilities at mushrooming institutions often have not caught up with the increased student population. This means that students who are forced to live outside the dormitories feel discriminated against, and tend to build up resentments and antagonisms which make them tense and restless. Sometimes overcrowding occurs which makes study difficult or limits privacy to an uncomfortable degree. Supervision and consultation may be inadequate because resident staff and advisers are spread too thin. In some colleges outside realtors have put up housing at a distance from the campus and these apartment buildings have only the most tenuous attachment to the college itself. The kind of closeness which fosters loyalty does not have a chance to develop under such circumstances. Students who do not feel cared for by their school are quick to criticize, and though they may be quite unaware of the underlying reasons for their hostility they are capable of expressing it loudly and violently at the slightest, sometimes imagined, provocation.

The Berkeley Crisis

The fateful combination of rising tension and resentment in the student body, plus an immediate concrete cause for righteous indignation, that occurred at the University of California at Berkeley in the fall of 1964 led to the most widely publicized demonstration so far experienced on a college campus.

An arbitrary ruling was made on September 14, 1964. This involved forbidding students to engage in recruiting or money-raising on the college grounds for any kind of political or civil rights organization. The action launched a series of student protests and disciplinary countermeasures by the administration which, by December, had escalated to a mass confrontation of the student body and the president of the university, with the nation looking on in fascination and distress.

The elements which contributed to the difficulties at Berkeley are multiple, and though many commentators have been tempted to point at one individual, or specific factors such as the student-faculty ratio or the large size of the institution, there is no simple answer. A potentially explosive atmosphere was present. The university had grown fast and there were a large number of young graduate students holding important teaching positions. The San Francisco area harbors a polyglot younger population. Many college age men and women gravitate there looking for opportunities which they think have been unavailable to them elsewhere. California is the last stopping place for many who have traveled westward from city to city looking for schools or jobs that have appeal. Such individuals tend to congregate around a university, finding companionship with others of the same age and interests. They do not feel any loyalty to the institution but rather reinforce the rebellious and critical feelings of the students, and play upon the wish of some to change whatever elements they may be dissatisfied with at the moment.

Also, in the fall of 1964 there were many critical issues in the air, not only civil rights but a national election in which

California was particularly involved. This of course played a much greater role in this state university than it would have in a privately controlled one. Whether political motives actually operated is unknown, but the students thought they did and at least they appear to have had grounds for such thoughts.

Into such a tinderbox was thrown a glowing spark in the form of the arbitrary ruling of September 14. Such a drastic restriction seemed unreasonable and proved to be so, yet it might have been accepted if mutual discussion had preceded its announcement. Probably the administration would have altered its plan if wider consultation about its fairness had been sought. At any rate the students would not have been left out of the discussion. As it was they felt insulted and rejected. When the original ruling was adjusted they still felt snubbed, for once again they had not been included to any significant degree in the planning of the adjustment. This continuing resentment about being ignored, as well as their beginning doubts about the unanimity of the administration's position, led to the testing of the new ruling, first by purposeful violation and then by the demand that 400 offenders be punished rather than the eight arbitrarily cited. This sort of "mass martyrdom" is a familiar maneuver and one that only a united administrative body which is in good communication with its student body can cope with. The interim without demonstrations was ushered in by the appearance of a new authority (President Clark Kerr) with a promise to discuss with all parties before making further rules. Here at last seemed to be a strong and a reasonable authority figure. But disappointment followed when the discussions he instituted failed to bring results. Again protest was heard and authority (this time the Regents) had to speak firmly and definitely. It did so by reinstating the eight and taking a clear stand in favor of student fund-raising and recruitment within the limits of the law; but this clearly stated stand was weakened and confused by the chancellor's notification of future disciplinary action against several of the reinstated students. This demonstration of uncertainty and lack of administrative solidarity led to an ultimatum and subsequent mass sit-in.

Two elements which run through this case history of student insurrection are significant. First, there was a failure to communicate about policy changes with those who were to be most affected by them. Advance warning and discussion, along with the enlistment of student cooperation in regard to the promulgation and enforcement of the new rules, would undoubtedly have prevented the trouble. Second, contradictory and irresolute attitudes on the part of the authorities involved gave the students an impression of weakness which both disappointed and delighted them. Their disappointment was expressed by anger, and their delight by a triumphant overriding of the apparently weakened adversary. But the victory, if it had come, would have been an unwelcome one. College students want limits set and they want to be proud of their leaders. Alex Braiman, psychiatrist at the University of Rochester, puts it well in an unpublished paper, "Riotous Behavior in the College Student" when he states:

Achieving a cohesive sense of identity involves . . . identification with models that are admired for their competence and style. In their efforts to be permissive too many of the elders in the institutions have merely become pallid, ambivalent or ambiguous, rendering the students' struggle for self-definition more difficult.

Firmness and reasonableness would seem to be the key words in dealing with controversial matters. At Brandeis when students protested a new rule about doors being kept open during women's visiting hours in men's dormitories and threatened a mass strike, President Sachar announced that all striking students, no matter how many in number, would be immediately suspended, and in the same statement granted permission for the students to present their complaints about the rule to the university's board of trustees. Similarly, President Brewster at Yale used firmness combined with reasonableness when the students protested the withholding of tenure from a faculty member. He announced that students should have no control over faculty appointments, but agreed to request a review of this decision by the committee responsible, making it clear at the same time that he would support whatever decision this group made after its review of the matter.

Authorities who deal with adolescents must be aware of the difference between the expressed need of the individual and the felt need. One is often quite the opposite of the other. College students may seem to be demanding complete freedom from restrictions of all kinds and to be out to destroy those who have made the rules and regulations. In reality they are testing the strength of an authority for which on a deep level they feel a great need and which they want to respect. An administration in touch with its undergraduate body can understand this double message and can react appropriately to the contradictory inner and outer demands of the student body. Firmness satisfies the inner need to be controlled, while explanation and discussion satisfy the outer and more frequently expressed need to be treated as responsible, intelligent adults. Students treated with respect and granted the degree of freedom and responsibility for which they are ready will respond by giving respect in return, and will profit in terms of their own individual personality development from the example of elders who are concerned and at the same time wise and resolute.

CHAPTER 6

Emotional Problems

Poverty, war, and the fear of both contributed to the psychological problems of earlier generations. Our present affluence can be turned to good use in the prevention and treatment of psychological illness in ways that were not possible in times of depression or war. Counseling and psychiatric services in colleges were almost unknown forty years ago. Now they are common, though they are by no means considered essential by all administrators. Yale was the pioneer in the field, not because it was more plagued by disturbed students than any other institution but rather by chance. Clements Fry, a physician with rare perceptiveness and sensitivity, happened to be a member of the medical staff there. Recognizing the need of many students for help and guidance, he started a clinic devoted to the promotion of mental health within that community over thirty years ago. Other universities, notably Harvard, the University of California at Berkeley, Minnesota, and Pennsylvania have followed his lead.

Some college presidents have expressed skepticism about this rapidly spreading attention to the emotional needs of students. One put it this way: "We never had any students with problems until we hired a psychiatrist." Another said, "The more cops in a town, the more criminals. It is the same way with psychiatrists and neurotics." These statements seem as logical as proclaiming that there were no bacteria until the microscope discovered them. Students in college have always been troubled, and because their problems were unrecognized and untreated there undoubtedly were more students a few decades ago who became seriously or permanently ill, who left college for good, or who committed suicide. Statistics to support this are hard to obtain, for no one keeps records about these forms of student behavior in universities where there is no mental health service. But most college officials and physicians in universities with adequate counseling services realize that many students each year remain at their studies and adjust more happily and productively to college life because of the help they receive from those who are trained to counsel and to treat the illnesses which so commonly occur in students of this age.

The proportion of college students who seek help for emotional problems is surprisingly consistent. Institutions of very different types find that 10 to 20 per cent of a graduating class have sought help for emotional problems at one time or another during the four undergraduate years. This ratio has varied little over the years, and has been reported by such diverse universities as Harvard, McGill, University of California, and University of British Columbia. It may seem uneconomical to spend so much time, money, and thought on such a small proportion of students; but it must be remembered that an understanding of the problems of this group can lead to recommendations for preventive measures which will assist the many who suffer but do not become ill. Also, some of those who have benefited from treatment have later on been the most distinguished in their class.

Pressures in college today are greater than ever before. The competition in high school for entrance to a prestige college, and the importance attached to higher education by parents and by business firms, impinge on the secondary school student so strongly that he is often exhausted by the time he arrives at the college which finally chooses him. Once there, he finds the demands different in nature as well as greater in degree than ten years ago. Almost immediately on arrival he is asked to make a number of choices in areas which are new to him. These demands and choices may not be very different today than they have always been, but the urgency the student feels in regard to meeting them and making the best decisions is quite new. Entrance to graduate school, or graduation itself with its ticket of admission to a respectable or profitable job, may depend on the rightness of a single choice or the perseverance to hang on through one more day of a grueling examination period. The vital importance of gaining a college degree is one of many unnecessary pressures placed upon our undergraduates by our present-day society.

Students have also been made to feel that there is a great hurry to get the business of education over with. Early admissions, advanced placement, and opportunities to take the senior year of college while enrolled in a graduate school all transmit a message of haste, rather than the atmosphere of quiet contemplation which is so conducive to learning and toward putting this learning to constructive use.

Despite the obvious relevance of these environmental college pressures, much more important is the strength and character of the individual student who must cope with these new stresses or else be defeated by them. Healthy personality development results from healthy influences from home, church, and school. The elements from these areas of his experience have been discussed earlier. Because they are less effective today, many emotional problems result from the vulnerability of the individual rather than the force of external pressure.

APATHY

In the midst of what would seem to be the most exciting of opportunities—intellectual, athletic, social, and political—some students find themselves becoming steadily more bored and lethargic. As each possibility for gaining new knowledge or experiencing a challenging responsibility appears upon the horizon, these students retreat deeper into solitude and introspection. They find less and less reason to be alive, and often reach the point where they give up eating as well as bathing. Sometimes the beginning of such a downward spiral coincides with a disappointment in grades or a love affair that fizzles, but more often it cannot be correlated with any specific event. It may even start after a notable success.

A college junior, for example, came for help in the midst of a period of apathy the beginning of which he dated to the return of a paper he had written about Ernest Hemingway on which he had received an "A." He had felt no elation on seeing his grade, although it was at least a whole letter higher than he had expected. That night he had consumed a great deal of whiskey in his room alone and uncharacteristically had become tearful and depressed as he drank, rather than exhilarated. After this night of overindulgence he felt extremely tired for several days; he attributed this to a bad hangover. He used this as an excuse for not attending classes or doing assignments for a week or so, but finally came to the medical clinic "for a checkup," and finding no answer, went on to the psychiatric clinic to see if someone there could restore his lost enthusiasm.

His history revealed that he was the oldest of three children all of whom had done very well in school, particuarly the middle brother who was a freshman at the same college. The father was a hard-driving, successful surgeon and the mother a socially ambitious clubwoman. Success had been in the atmosphere at home all his life and he had not broken this tradition until now. He was well on his way toward a career in medicine and seemed at home in the social set deemed desirable by his mother. His relationships with girls had been superficial but seemingly satisfying. There appeared to be nothing traumatic in his life history, past or current, that could account for this sudden flagging of interest.

This student's general behavior differed from that of a good many others afflicted with apathy only in that he retained a modicum of conscience—enough to move him to seek help and understanding. He remained in treatment for several months, during which some alarming facts came out. One was that he was regularly driving his sports car in the early hours of the morning at dangerous speeds around city rotaries and down narrow country roads. Twice he had skidded off the road, and once had overturned. Another was that he had, in the last week before coming to the clinic, seriously contemplated shooting himself. Not as alarming but surprising were other facts previously unknown even to the student himself. These related to his underlying fears about becoming a doctor, and his feelings of relative inferiority to his younger brother, with consequent strong jealousy and hatred. He was also concerned about being impotent in the sexual relationship which he felt might grow out of any deep emotional commitment to a girl. It is easy to understand, with these latter facts in mind, why this student might be afraid to compete and wish simply to fade away from the challenge of studies and social activities. Perhaps studying Hemingway for his paper reinforced feelings of concern about proving his strength and virility, as well as suggesting violent death and suicide; but of this we can be less sure. At any rate the pressure of overbearing parents, college requirements, and the demands which he felt were being made by his peers for proof of sexual adequacy combined to break down his ability to cope. But the collapse probably would not have occurred had developmental influences provided this student with strength enough to resist the pressures. A chance to prove his adequacy earlier in life, hardships overcome in childhood, and a chance to act on his own even against parental wishes when a younger adolescent might have enabled him to develop the strength necessary to cope successfully in college.

The problem of apathy does not affect only those from the professional or upper classes. A Negro from a Pennsylvania coal mining town was admitted to college with support by a foundation interested in enlarging opportunities for the underprivileged. He stood at the top of his high school class, was a star athlete, and had won medals for sportsmanship and "high moral character." At college he was never able to "get going." Despite hours spent with books in his room and in the library, he simply could not learn the material. It became increasingly difficult for him to write papers for his freshman English course, and he felt compelled to give up football in a desperate effort to find more time for his studies. His adviser realized that the boy was achieving far below his capacity in spite of valiant effort, and sent him for psychological counseling. At first, attempts to evaluate the situation were thwarted by sullen silence, denials that anything was really upsetting to him, and promises to "do better next week," but eventually a long story of unhappiness came pouring out. This student had always wanted to work on a farm and to lead what appeared to him to be an uncomplicated life, but pressure from family, school, and sponsoring foundation as well as officials in his home town and his high school had persuaded him to accept the opportunity offered to go North and avail himself of further education. Solving the problems of adjusting to a totally different environment represented more of an effort than he was able or willing to make, yet he could not tell this to anyone. He could only make his point by failing to pass his courses. The disgrace of flunking out seemed less threatening to him than that of refusing to accept the privilege offered to him originally.

Not all surgeons' sons or foundation-sponsored Negro students have as serious a problem with apathy as did these two, but the examples illustrate the effect that powerful cultural forces can have on individuals unable to fulfill real or fancied expectations. Often outward appearances belie the internal state of mind, for such pressured individuals may perform well but feel as though their achievements are based on good luck or the mistaken opinion of others. Basically they feel unworthy and incapable.

DISHONESTY

Cheating in college was thrown into the limelight fairly recently at the time of the nomination and election of a United States Congressman. Some surprise was shown that a student who had let a classmate take an exam for him would be allowed to return to college after one year's suspension. Yet this is standard practice at many universities. The fear of expulsion and permanent ruin of a career is no longer a deterrent to dishonesty in most colleges. Plagiarizing, stealing books from libraries, and wanton destruction of property are offenses familiar to all deans. In these days when any threat to graduation should seem especially to be avoided, it is surprising at first glance to find so many undergraduates in this sort of trouble. Closer and deeper observation of individual cases, however, shows that most offenses of this kind spring either from an incomplete or distorted (sometimes termed "corrupted") development of conscience, or else are means unconsciously adopted by students to extract themselves from untenable situations.

Conscience building begins in early childhood, as has been described in a previous chapter. This rudimentary regulator remains as a steadying and basic guiding influence through the teens with their stormy rebellious phases. In college, when the process of identity formation requires a casting aside of what are felt to be superimposed values, the earlier formed conscience still is effective. College students whose conscience development has been normal may speak in alarming (to their parents) ways about free love and communism, but their actual behavior is limited by their conscience to prevent acting in a manner that will cause guilt or unhappiness. The words they utter may sound violent and undisciplined but only rarely does destructive action follow.

Those whose consciences have not been well formed in childhood and are not reinforced by church and school in later adolescence often find themselves swept into dishonest and even criminal behavior. Such students are more likely to cheat or steal when placed in an untenable situation from which there seems to be no exit, but even those with a strongly disciplined upbringing occasionally cannot overcome a compulsion, when they feel trapped, to break rules so blatantly and so obviously that exposure is inevitable. This represents an attempt sometimes to bring punishment or disgrace upon themselves as a way to expiate guilt over some fancied crime, or else ensure being fired from college to escape the responsibility and consequences of graduation.

A college senior was apprehended by the police on complaint of his roommate for forging endorsements on checks stolen from the roommate's desk drawer. The amount of deceptiveness was so small and the attempts to cover up so few that the "crime" could not have failed to be discovered. The police felt that the case should be handled by the college authorities, and released the student to the custody of the dean. There was no previous history of this sort of behavior, and no reason to believe that any unusual stress was present in the boy's life at the time of the forgeries. His academic standing was high and he had been accepted by a top-notch graduate school. Such uncharacteristic behavior seemed to the dean to indicate serious emotional illness. He referred the student to the counseling center for evaluation before deciding what to do administratively.

After a series of interviews and psychological testing a rather typical picture emerged. The boy had grown up in a wealthy middle-class family. His father was a real estate operator. His mother had come from humble origins, and had been catapulted into the highly competitive social world of her husband's friends and business colleagues with suddenness and considerable reluctance. Although emphasis in this group was put on being respectable, there was double-dealing and shading of the truth beneath the surface. Various business manipulations—many of them verging on blackmail—were discussed by the father within the family circle. At the same time the mother used white lies with frequency and proficiency to cover up embarrassing details from her past and to move into or out of social engagements. Psychological tests showed that this student's conscience had been so corrupted by the dishonesty and insincerity prevalent at home that it did not reinforce the traditional standards of morality to a normal degree. His conscience was less well prepared than it should have been to help him at a time of stress.

In addition, there were factors present that did not appear in any current records and were relevant to the acts of forgery. Two weeks previously the student had received a letter from his mother saying that she was leaving immediately for Reno to obtain a divorce. Talk of separation had been fairly frequent in the course of family disputes over the past several years, but none of the children had ever seriously faced the possibility that it could become a reality. Learning that his mother had decided to give up on her marriage in such an abrupt manner had upset this student. It had stirred up within him feelings of rage against his mother that surprised and concerned him. His first impulse had been to rush home and keep her from leaving, but he did not do so because of a fear that he would explode with rage and harm her. Instead he suppressed his anger and allowed it to simmer.

At the time of the forgeries he was coping with another stress, also. He had been involved to a limited degree with a girl from his home town. She had recently begun to care much more strongly for him than he for her, but he had allowed the relationship to continue and indeed had fostered it. He had enjoyed the power he maintained over her. A week or so before he stole the checks, he had become either bored or disgusted with her behavior—he could not tell which—and had stopped corresponding with her. On the night before the first forgery she had telephoned him in a desperate frame of mind. She was exceedingly depressed and had threatened suicide.

In this instance, a student plagued by unconscious feelings of guilt and anger reacted in a neurotic and uncharacteristic way. He punished himself for having hurt his girl, and struck out against his mother for having deserted the family, by putting himself in serious disciplinary trouble. Equipped with a stronger or less confused conscience, he might well have found a less self-destructive way out of his dilemma.

The unconscious use of dishonesty as a way to resolve what appears on the surface to be an insoluble conflict is familiar to all who work in a counseling relationship with students. Sometimes a girl attending a coeducational college will find herself pushed by faculty and family to utilize the education she has been given by going on to graduate school and not "waste" it by becoming a wife and mother. The girl herself, on the other hand, may be experiencing strong internal pressure toward marriage. Obligation to family (both financial and moral) plus intellectual interest pull one way, while love and maternal instinct pull the other. Sometimes a workable and rational compromise may be possible, but often a surprising event such as an "unplanned" pregnancy, an elopement, a sudden failure, or a dishonest act such as plagiarism occurs instead.

SUICIDE AND DEPRESSION

The possibility of suicide lurks at the back of the mind of anyone dealing in any degree of depth with adolescents. Mood swings are so rapid and unexplainable that one fears that at almost any moment suicidal impulses might arise and be acted upon. Adolescence is a time when death holds a high degree of fascination. It is something to be curious about and to experiment with. Yet to the rest of us it seems to be the most tragic age to die. Actually the statistics are reassuring;

suicides in younger adolescents (twelve to seventeen) are exceedingly rare and usually occur within the context of severe mental illness. The exceptions are those children who kill themselves out of defiance, usually without meaning to, in order to "make them sorry they did that to me."

Even in older adolescents the national suicide rate is well below half that for the population at large. However, colleges that conscientiously report and investigate student illnesses and deaths show a figure for suicide considerably higher than the national average for this age. The student health service at Berkeley recently published a paper confirming this difference, which may indicate that college is an environment conducive to depression and suicide, or perhaps that individuals more likely to kill themselves choose to go to college. There is no concrete evidence to support statements made recently to the effect that suicides are increasing in greater proportion than the increasing number of students; but college health workers generally note a trend toward more suicidal attempts in their student populations over the past five years. The fact that girls make such attempts twice as frequently as men, while men successfully commit suicide three times as often as girls, is as true in the student group as it is in the general population.

The college student who takes his own life is usually suffering from one of three things: a seriously upsetting mental illness (schizophrenia or manic depressive psychosis), neurotic illness involving a plea for help which is miscalculated, or deep depression. The first type of student is hard to identify as a suicidal risk. He may be acting bizarrely or attracting attention in some way, but he rarely indicates his preoccupation with suicide even though he may be planning it in the most intricate detail. One such student was a sophomore who had been in treatment since early in his freshman year. He had been troubled by weird fantasies and had irrational suspicions about what people thought of him. All of this he shared with his doctor but to his classmates he seemed normal. He was doing well in his studies and appeared to be under no unusual stress, until one day he told his doctor very matter of factly that he was planning to shoot himself that night. He could give no specific reason for killing himself but expressed a wish to do something dramatic and unexpected. The fact that he would not be able to witness the effects of this specific act did not deter him, although he was curious about the length of time he would remain conscious after the bullet had penetrated his skull. Clearly this suicidal impulse, which he fortunately was willing to reveal to his doctor, originated in the deranged portion of the boy's mind. He was hospitalized for his own protection, and several months later was grateful for having been rescued.

Suicidal gestures made in an attempt to gain attention and sympathy or to signal for help sometimes misfire and lead to death. While this is rare in first attempts, it is much less so on second and third attempts. Every suicidal gesture must be taken seriously and treated as an indication that something is wrong and needs prompt attention.

Sometimes it is difficult to face up to the responsibility imposed by a suicidal move. For example, during Christmas vacation of her freshman year a girl enrolled at a highly competitive college was found deeply asleep at four in the afternoon on the day she was to return to school. An open bottle of sleeping pills one-quarter full was on the bedtable. Her family was an unsophisticated one living in a small farming town. Dealing with an attempted suicide was too much for this widowed mother, and she chose to pretend that nothing out of the ordinary had happened. She poured coffee into her daughter and carried her onto the evening train which took her back to college 2,000 miles away. She did not inform anyone at home or at the university about what had happened. Two nights later the girl died from an overdose of sleeping pills—the quarter bottle which her mother had packed for her, plus another whole bottle obtained illegally from a drugstore near the campus.

No one enjoys facing up to the fact that a friend or relative is on the verge of suicide. It is unpleasant enough in itself, but it also makes a demand upon the person who knows to accept responsibility and to take action—usually action of a difficult and often embarrassing sort. Yet it is important that these calls for help be heeded. Sometimes it is just a way of saying that school or college is too hard, or that others in the family have been receiving more attention—simple things which often can be easily changed. This dramatic way of communicating such minor concerns may, in some families and college communities, seem to be the only way to get a message through. If the method backfires and brings a reaction of anger and further withdrawal from those to whom the appeal is made, then all hope seems gone.

Apathy, dishonesty, and suicide are only three of the many problems students bring to college mental health clinics. Depression, phobias, and sexual problems also occur frequently among the undergraduates but are not as specific to this age group. Counseling or psychiatric services are needed to help the young men and women in our colleges and graduate schools resolve these problems. Equally important, however, is the development of a counseling attitude on the part of faculty, administration, and parents. This should include an understanding of the nature of the internal as well as the external struggles that complicate the life of the young in today's world. Such a counseling attitude toward students and their problems can prevent the development of symptoms which need more professional treatment; it can also lead to the earlier recognition of these same symptoms when they do occur, and to an appropriate referral.

CHAPTER 7

Religion

Next to training and guidance provided within the home, the most important contribution to the development of a healthy personality is a faith. Unfortunately, spokesmen for the church have so watered down the spiritual element in religion that what once was a deeply moving and effective guiding force has come to be regarded by many young people of high school and college age as simply another philosophical or psychological approach to life, one which can be argued about in the same pragmatic terms as the choice of a career or the relative merits of brands of cigarettes. Dedication and fervent commitment have been increasingly replaced by rationalistic and intellectual internal debate. The "leap into faith" so essential to the achievement of a meaningful religious life is made more and more difficult for young people by the prevalent attempts to explain by scientific logic—often in the most inappropriate jargonistic psychological terms—what is meant to transcend everyday rationality. The men in the church who have lost the courage of their spiritual convictions have thus deprived a significant group of young people of the guidance and inspiration they desperately need.

A study of 500 college students reported by Gordon Allport in his book *The Individual and His Religion* does much to refute the current popular concept that college students are not affected by religion. He found that 82 per cent of his Harvard and Radcliffe sample felt that for maturity of personality religion is required. Seven out of ten regarded themselves as actually or potentially religious. This is hard to reconcile with the statement reported by the Rev. H.O.J. Brown in his aritcle in the June 1965 *National Review* entitled "The Protestant Deformation." He quoted a college chaplain as stating, "You're talking to Harvard and Radcliffe students. If you want them to listen, you can't talk about God."

Some observers point to the recent rapprochment between religion and psychiatry as a cause of the secularization of religion. While this may have some validity, it does not need to have, for the approaches of each toward the alleviation of suffering are quite different. One discipline can gain inspiration and ideas from the other, but total amalgamation would destroy both. The degree to which one can use the concepts and the tools of the other is difficult to define, but this needs to be done in the context of mutual respect—not with an attitude of competition on an academic or social level. Religionists sometimes speak of themselves as second-class citizens in the area of helping people, and talk as though psychotherapists had the *true* answer for the cure of emotional ills. This feeling of inferiority is not helped by the expressed attitudes of therapists who derogate religion and perpetuate the myth that intelligent people with problems do not find solutions in religion but rather from psychiatry. Intelligence is no bar to religious faith, nor is it always an aid to health through psychotherapy—sometimes the intellect may even be a barrier to the achievement of insight. The effects of religious belief in preventing emotional breakdown as well as in restoring mental health should be more widely studied and reported on by scientists. The few studies as yet done indicate that religion can have both a preventive and a therapeutic effect on neurotic symptoms.

RELIGION AND PERSONALITY DEVELOPMENT

Religion can begin to become a powerful factor in the development of personality in early childhood. Sunday school, worship services, and parents' references to God register sharply on a child's mind and play an important part in reinforcing prohibitions and expectations. The added dimension provided by a religious context gives greater depth of meaning to standards and values taught by parents and school. Hope of a life hereafter and the fear of divine punishment, as well as present communication with a spiritual father, are building stones for the growth and development of a healthy conscience which are equally as important as parental reprimands and rewards. A clearcut stand on morality, transmitted through the voice of the clergy and the interpretation of

Scripture, can lay a foundation of basic morality which may enable a youngster to withstand the inevitable *sturm und drang* of adolescence with far less distress.

When the natural rebelliousness of the teen-age years sets in, the church must be ready to deal with it. The temporary rejection at this age of what a young person feels to have been superimposed by parents often includes giving up church attendance and profession of atheism or agnosticism. Sometimes the opposite occurs. Adolescents, particularly girls, may have a conversion experience at this time and undergo an intensification of religious feeling or become deeply involved in a faith different from that in which they were brought up. In instances where such a change is not made simply out of rebellion, such experiences can be made use of by parents and pastors with encouragement to follow through, not treated as isolated incidents which the individual will "get over."

Surveys indicate there are a large number of religiously accessible young people in the college group. Encouraging them to look upon religious experience as a discovery will enable these open-minded and independent thinking young people to accept spiritual satisfaction and religious guidance as a new and important element in their lives. Such an approach directed at this group specifically can prevent them from feeling that they are simply following the old patterns devised for them at home when they were children. This has been done successfully with teen-agers in many parishes, and by larger church organizations such as DeMolay, Hillel, and the Catholic Youth Organization. Some similar groups have, by diluting the spiritual too much with the secular, failed to take advantage of the latent religious interest of the young. Athletics, drama, and dance groups may replace worship and religious discussion as the principal activity. Such innovations are often made to broaden the membership and include many who have no real religious interest. The group might be more effective if it left this lukewarm minority to their own devices and concentrated instead on strengthening the faith of those for whom it has real meaning.

PSYCHIATRIC AND RELIGIOUS VIEWS OF MAN

The psychiatric and religious viewpoints on the individual and his adjustment to the world around him are different. The approach of the former is primarily internal, the latter external; but the goals are similar in that both the therapist and the religionist are attempting to help another person, one a sick patient and the other a healthy parishioner, to understand himself better in the context of the world at large. The internal structure of man is not conceived very differently by the two disciplines, though their vocabularies are indeed distinct.

Freud's concept of the unconscious, described by him as "a chaos of seething excitement which knows no values, no good and evil, no morality," does not differ very much from the "sinful desires of the flesh" mentioned in a Protestant baptismal service. The irrational force of the Id which compels one to behave in a manner contrary to one's better judgment is also well described in the Bible by St. Paul when he says, "If I do what I would not, it is no more I that do it but sin that dwelleth in me; for I delight in the law of God after the inward man, but I see another law in my members warring against the law of my mind."

In oversimplified language the nature of man, whether viewed in religious or psychiatric terms, makes it difficult for him to control himself and behave in a way that appears rational and reasonable from his own as well as society's point of view. He needs help, sometimes simply as an ordinary citizen trying to go about his business in a sensible fashion, and sometimes as a patient crippled by neurotic symptoms. He looks outside himself for assistance in controlling his impulses, strengthening his will, sorting out what is real from what is imagined, and gaining perspective on life as a whole, in terms of meaning and purpose and what his own individual goals and ambitions should be.

The psychiatrist has little to offer the healthy individual seeking answers to questions about the meaning of life. Attempts to interpret the needs of healthy people from the study of the ill have not proved fruitful as yet. Despite much study about the ideal emotional and physical climate for child rearing, not many helpful rules have been forthcoming. In spite of much study in the area of delinquency, no clear answer about prevention has yet been produced. Most of the world still looks to its religious leaders as guides to harmonious and satisfying living.

DISTINCTIONS BETWEEN RELIGIOUS AND PSYCHOLOGICAL COUNSELING

In dealing with emotionally disturbed individuals there emerges a distinct difference between the attitudes of ministers and psychiatrists. The psychiatrist tries to help by bringing about internal changes which enable the patient to adapt better to his environment. The main emphasis is on the person in trouble helping himself by being willing to face up to feelings or memories within his unconscious which formerly he was avoiding. The religious counselor on the other hand helps the individual to view his problems within the context of his religion and to bear his suffering or to resolve it through the help of an external agent. He may make unavoidable suffering more bearable through solace achieved by prayer, or relieve guilt by confession, absolution, or penance.

A case in point is that of a graduate student who was greatly concerned over homosexual experiences that had occurred during the early years of his adolescence, and a continuing rare attraction to contemporary males which while not strictly sexual seemed to him abnormally strong. He came from a distinguished family; his father was a diplomat and his mother an internationally famous hostess. He had three older brothers all of whom had done well in some professional field. This student underwent psychotherapy on a moderately intensive basis for over a year. He was a cooperative patient and came to understand the origins of his homosexual tendencies rather early in treatment. His remoteness from his father was made extreme not only by the parent's work abroad for the State Department but also by a coolness stemming from the father's knowledge that the boy was not his natural son but the issue of one of his mother's affairs with another man. This rejection, coupled with a harsh peremptory attitude assumed by his mother, had made the student more than usually isolated and lonely. From the age of eight he had been attending Episcopal services, having been introduced to the church by an Anglican governess. There he had gained a feeling of belonging which had partially filled the emotional void.

In the course of therapy, a number of important insights were gained. The causes for this man's unusual concern about past sexual "transgressions" as well as the reason for his having become involved in homosexual practices in the first place were well delineated. Although the achievement of such insights usually helps bring about the amelioration or disappearance of symptoms, such did not occur in this case. When the therapist probed more deeply into the religious life of this patient, he found that there had been an abandonment of the church over the last four years. The student had felt that his past sins made him no longer acceptable as a participant in either the religious or the social events of his church.

It was only after his confession and absolution within the church that significant progress was made in overcoming this man's original symptoms. Once his relationship with God was re-established and his feeling of being an integral part of a church community had been restored, he was once again a whole enough person emotionally to move beyond his homosexual attachments.

RELIGION AS A "NEUROSIS"

Religion as an ingredient of healthy adjustment has been criticized by some psychiatrists as representing a crutch which is detrimental because it deprives the individual of complete self-reliance and self-expression. The antagonism to psychiatry engendered by this point of view (one which is falsely attributed to many psychiatrists) is reinforced by Freud's 1927 paper, "The Future of an Illusion." In this essay he termed religion a "mass neurosis." He equated religious believers with those who are infantile and unable to break outgrown ties with their parents. Freud was not as dogmatic and arbitrary as many believe, for in this same paper he wrote:

I know how difficult it is to avoid illusions. Perhaps even the hopes I have confessed to are of an illusory nature, but I hold fast to one distinction. My illusions are not, like the religious ones, incapable of correction. They have no delusional character. If experience should show, not to me but to others after me that think as I do, that we are mistaken, then we shall give up our expectations.

Time has indeed brought many changes in the thinking of important men in the fields of psychiatry and psychology. While it may be premature to say that the Freudians should make good on their master's promise and admit they "are mistaken," some of their present spokesmen do voice a far different opinion. Carl Jung has written, in a description of his patients over the age of thirty-five, "all have been people whose problem in the last resort was that of finding a religious outlook on life." Gordon Allport, one of the Harvard's most distinguished professors of psychology, writes: "Many personalities attain a religious view of life without suffering arrested development and without self-deception. Indeed it is by virtue of their religious outlook on life—expanding as experience expands—that they are able to build and maintain a mature and well-integrated edifice of personality"; and again: "A man's religion . . . is his ultimate attempt to enlarge and to complete his own personality by finding the supreme context in which he rightly belongs."

There are many healthy individuals for whom religion is unnecessary and who indeed are so constituted that the "leap into faith" is impossible. Religion is rarely effective as a solace, guide, or inspiration if it is forced upon a person; but for those who can open themselves to the emotional acceptance of faith in a person or a force greater than man, there comes an added dimension which may spell the difference between emotional health and emotional illness.

THE NEW MORALITY

If religion is "to build and maintain a mature and a well-integrated edifice of personality" and to help man find "the supreme context in which he rightly belongs," must it not provide him with ethical guidelines that are consistent? The "new morality" does not seem to provide these, and in fact is so contradictory and "soft" that it would appear to break down the natural restraints of conscience rather than maintain or reinforce them. Essentially this modern religious approach to morality seems to separate ethics from Scripture and to interpret good and evil strictly in terms of love—a word broadly and variously defined in both lay and religious language. It is this very deep confusion about the definition of love which makes the new morality virtually useless as a system of ethics.

John Robinson, Bishop of Woolwich, writes, "I recognize to the full that all of us, especially young people, have to have working rules. But my point is that when these are questioned as they are being questioned the Christian is driven back to base them not on law ('Fornication is always wrong') but on love, on what deep concern for persons as whole persons, in their entire social context, really requires." This basically says that while young people need rules they cannot have them, instead they must make up their own rules for each individual situation involving another person on the basis of that person's "entire social context." For a person with any degree of concern, such a decision would take an endless amount of research of the most clinical and unloving sort. It could hardly be made in the midst of passion.

Robinson further confuses the situation with the statement, "They must decide *for themselves* though this certainly does not mean that they must decide on their own. They should not be loaded with the burden of decision alone. Nevertheless the church cannot take it *from* them." This kind of double talk cannot gain the respect of our younger generation. Surveys show that college students have a respect for traditional religion. They admire those who stand for an absolute morality, even though they reserve the right to question it in their own rationalistic manner and even to mock it. Anyone who has watched a group of young people at a religious discussion knows the inaccuracy of Bishop Robinson's statement, "And supranaturalist reasons—that God or Christ has pronounced it 'a sin'—have force and even meaning for none but a diminishing religious remnant." It is likely that the non-believers are more vocal than the believers, and perhaps this has led the bishop to think that the latter are a "remnant" of the population. Surely the churches will not be able to help those who most need strength and guidance by following this wobbly line. And whom will they attract? Certainly not the disbelievers, who already profess no need for direction or ethical principles other than their own logic.

The religious proponents of greater sexual freedom may be

mistaking the exhibitionistic proclamations of a few for the general view of the majority and, as the Rev. H. O. J. Brown suggests, making "it quite plain that their principal reason for wanting to revise Christian standards is that nobody likes them today." Such a swing in the wind of changing social mores is not consonant with church tradition. Moral practices have swung in many contrary directions over the centuries but most people have been reassured to find religious principles remaining stable. It would be ironical if, upon the next swing of the weathercock, the church should find itself advocating greater license and promiscuity than the secular society around it. Perhaps it is even now in this position. One college chaplain in a recent sermon seemed to epitomize the situation when he said, "I turn out to be a conservative in this matter. I hold out for premarital chastity and lifelong marriages. I think sex is better that way. But I know there are many exceptions to both and I am issuing no blanket condemnations. There is only one absolute for a Christian—the love of God." Being for and against the same thing, admitting exceptions to every rule and calling upon "the love of God" as a moral regulator without interpreting it in usable terms, is hardly in the tradition of a church that has lived for centuries as an example and guide to mankind in the ways and means by which human beings can live in the best degree of harmony and happiness together.

Moral Responsibility

The psychiatrist in his work with patients having problems in the social area—delinquents, chronic liars, cheats, thieves—

needs to have society set limits on behavior. Otherwise his patient is unable to recognize an illness and embark upon its cure. Several years ago a divinity student was sent for psychiatric treatment by his dean because he had been apprehended by the college security officer while stealing books from the library. He had confessed to a two-year career of thievery and the dean in making the referral said to the psychiatrist, "He is obviously a sick man." Neither the dean nor the school made this explicit to the student, however, and after several months of rather desultory treatment the therapist asked his patient whether he really wanted to get over his illness. He received this startling reply: "Illness? I do not see that I am ill. I stole the books from the library and nothing has made me regret it. I am in good standing at school, have an opportunity to chat with a psychiatrist at no expense, and still have the money from selling the books. What is sick about that?" Here society, and in this case the church also, had failed to make clear to this individual that he had done wrong by their standards by reprimanding him for breaking the rules. This left him uncertain as to what indeed was right or wrong or sick or well.

Psychiatrists view antisocial behavior as symptomatic of an underlying illness and they focus on an attempt to cure this basic disturbance. They need not, and often cannot, be punitive or judicial, but to accomplish their aims they need to have cooperation from society through a clear definition of ethical standards and their enforcement. This does not mean that those in the field of psychiatry derogate or demean the forces which set and uphold the rules. On the contrary, the psychiatrist wants and often asks that churches, parents, schools, and law enforcement agencies clarify their rules and consistently back them up with a just system of punitive action. This not only aids in the treatment of the offender but can do much to prevent illness and misbehavior.

CHAPTER 8

Challenge

The younger generation has always presented a challenge to its elders. New times and new ideas make the environment unlike the one their parents coped with when they were young. This, plus the natural desire of children to be different from their fathers and mothers, makes the problem a new one for each generation of parents. Our present parent generation does not have the excuses that many past ones had. We cannot blame a war or a depression. Most of us are in a position to do anything and everything for our sons and daughters. In cases where this may not be economically possible, government agencies, private foundations, and scholarship programs are ready to step in and make up the difference. Given all these advantages, we are still dissatisfied with the results. What is expected of parents? How can they meet the challenge presented by the largest number of the healthiest and most intelligent young people in the history of our country?

In three areas our responsibility seems most clearly defined: being good models, citing facts out of our greater experience, and providing a challenge to the young so that they can feel their own strength through experiencing it. Once they have come to believe in it, they are able then to use it constructively.

Setting a good example as parents, teachers, doctors, politicians, and also as stage and screen heroes, is not an easy task. We are all limited by our own natural defects and inadequacies, but we should not be afraid to define and clarify our characters honestly. Our foibles are often reassuring to those who are struggling vainly to emulate us. Young men and women want to know where parents and teachers stand on social, academic, political, and moral issues. They need to sense strength and consistency in their elders, even if it is in defense of principles with which they cannot agree. Adolescents want authority to be defined; they become frightened when it is shadowy, vague, contradictory, or enigmatic. Sarcasm and insincerity make them feel depreciated and unrespected. To invite argument and to be willing to debate issues with the young leads them to feel worthwhile and to respect authority, though on the surface they may express strong disagreement.

MASS MEDIA

Examples and models do not come only from living people but are found increasingly in fictional characters in the theater, on the television screen, and in contemporary novels. It is important that we be aware of the considerable influence the mass media have on the developing standards and values of young people. Attitudes toward various kinds of sexual and social behavior are transmitted to the adolescent through a television program or a work of fiction much more convincingly than to an adult. The teen-ager is more alert to odd or sensational patterns of behavior and more ready to adopt them as his own than are his parents who see them as totally fictional—interesting perhaps but not to be imitated. Thus casual or revolutionary attitudes toward sex, when included in a play or a book which is highly praised by parents, are often mistakenly thought to represent attitudes shared by them and as praiseworthy as the work itself.

A good example of this sort of casualness can be found in Edward Albee's Pulitzer prize-winning play, *Who's Afraid of Virginia Woolf?* In one scene a guest at a college professor's home participates in a game called "Hump the Hostess." While adultery has been a common theme in all forms of literature, it has seldom been dealt with in such a matter of fact and amoral fashion. Adults enjoying such a play can be shocked or amused by this, but a younger person is likely to be considerably influenced in his or her own struggle with values by such representation of illicit sex as a parlor game of no apparent consequence.

A recent television program dealt with a school's attitude toward an unmarried student who became pregnant. The school officials were portrayed as villains because they took a moral stand about the girl's indiscretion, while those who accepted her behavior as normal (including the fact that she assumed no responsibility for the bringing up of the child) were portrayed as the heroes of the piece. This would appear to confirm Margaret Mead's statement that society today "condemns premarital intercourse and rewards premarital pregnancy."

PORNOGRAPHY

Censoring or restricting the publication and distribution of pornographic or obscene literature does not solve this problem. Such legislative action is extremely difficult largely because the words "pornographic" and "obscene" are almost impossible to define. In an excellent discussion of this subject which appeared as an article in the March 1965 issue of *Harper's Magazine*, George P. Elliott tries to define pornography as "the representation of directly or indirectly erotic acts with an intrusive vividness which offends decency without aesthetic justification," but then goes on to say that this does not help very much since decency then must be defined. He ends up by writing that pornography is "relative, an ambiguous matter of personal taste and the consensus of opinion."

Rather than trying to define pornography and obscenity and then legislate against them, it is more realistic and helpful to be reconciled to the continual presence in our literature of material designed to be shocking, extreme, and offensive, and to counteract the destructive influence this material may have on our children by frank discussion of our attitudes as parents and teachers. First we must know more specifically how the reading and viewing of this subject matter affects the attitudes and behavior of the young.

It is a matter of considerable controversy whether seeing or reading about sexual behavior, both normal and perverted, incites similar action on the part of the reader or observer, or whether it serves instead as a healthy outlet for fantasy and may actually prevent action rather than stimulate it. There is equal confusion over the possible harmfulness of the violence which plays such a large role in the Westerns on television and in the crime comic books. Certainly continuous exposure to "dirty" books and pictures can make sex become an obsession and could encourage experimentation which might lead to the development of perverted sexual habit patterns. Most young people only dabble in this kind of reading material, largely because it is forbidden and therefore attractively risky. Others may do so because their sexual knowledge is shockingly limited and pornography is the main source of information available to them.

Probably the most damaging element in current pornography is the manner in which sexual activity is described. Too much of what is written about sex makes it appear as a violent and antagonistic struggle instead of a tender, loving extra dimension to a deep emotional involvement. In *Fanny Hill*, for instance, each sexual relationship is described in terms which sound more like a military skirmish than a coming together for mutual pleasure. In the space of three pages in this book the male sexual organ is described as a "weapon," a "machine," "gristle," and a "stretcher," while female genitalia are labeled "fleshy excrescence," "deep flesh wound," and a "pleasure conduit." Sexual intercourse itself is recalled as "he bore and battered against me." Henry Miller, in two pages of *Tropic of Cancer*, talks about having intercourse in public, placing self-exploding rockets in the vagina, biting off parts of

the genitals, and plucking pubic hairs to paste them on someone's chin—all in angry tones and with plentiful use of four-
letter words. Such a passage can be read by adults either with
disgust and disbelief or with amusement at Miller's bawdy, in-
tentionally shocking humor; but adolescents are much more
impressionable, since their experience with sex as an expression of love has usually been slight. In the same way Norman
Mailer's preoccupation with the ecstasy of the orgasm can be
understood by adults as a ridiculous exaggeration, but for the
young it can lead to serious distortions in their concept of the
nature and spirit of the sexual act.

Some of the movies and plays produced today do present
sex in an attractive form. One of the best examples is the
recent movie of the classic novel *Tom Jones*. In this film sexual relationships are clearly good fun and indulged in for pure
pleasure without violence or shame. If the setting had been
contemporary rather than eighteenth century, it would have
given a false impression about the degree of casualness in our
current attitude toward fornication; but, as Elliott points out
in the article mentioned earlier, distance makes intimacy attractive while close examination of what may look attractive
from afar often destroys its beauty. The lighthearted attitude
toward sexual dalliance portrayed in *Tom Jones* cannot of
course be encouraged among the young, but the robust,
healthy sexual enjoyment so delightfully conveyed in this film
can be welcomed and hopefully made part of their licit sexual
relationships later in life.

What can be done to prevent the distortion and misconcep-
tions presented in some of our current literature from harm-
ing the developing attitudes toward sex in our adolescents?

First, the sale of such books to children under eighteen can be forbidden. This is as logical as keeping an inaccurate history book out of the classroom. Second, we can forearm the young with adequate information about sex so that those who do manage to obtain such books illegally (and many are bound to) will be aware of the pleasant aspects of sexuality and can weigh one set of attitudes against the other. And third, we must know enough about these books, plays, and television programs to be prepared for intelligent discussion of them and thus be able to counteract, through the expression of our own attitudes, their influence on our children. We must know the nature of the enemy if we are to oppose him effectively.

FACTS AND CHALLENGE

Our second major responsibility to the younger generation is to present them with facts—not simply about sex but about many other aspects of life. While the adolescent can learn many lessons only through his own experience, there are matters about which he will take advice, or at least think about more carefully and deeply, if he is presented with information other than what he can pick up from contemporaries or his own reading and observation.

The statistics on automobile accidents occurring after drinking, deaths from lung cancer in heavy smokers, unwanted pregnancies, and the frequency of addiction must become part of the everyday knowledge of each person growing up today. Yet preaching, scolding, and threatening usually fail to accomplish this. Within the context of a discussion at home, in school, or church much of this meaty material can be offered in digestible and retainable form. When the young are allowed to air their views freely and in an atmosphere where they are not afraid of being ridiculed, criticized, or raising the wrath of the elders present, they find that there is not as much unanimity among themselves as they had at first imagined, and they also often discover that the elders are not as rigid and as conservative as they had appeared. This atmosphere of mutual curiosity and sharing of opinions is conducive to learning. Usually at the end of such a discussion everyone leaves with some new knowledge and perhaps a few changed ideas.

Providing Challenge

The final major responsibility is that of providing a challenge for our adolescents—a means by which they can prove and test themselves against their contemporaries and the world at large. Some contend that today's fight for grades is the greatest challenge any younger generation has ever had to face, but this competition is not what most of the young are seeking. In the first place, it is a purely intellectual challenge and not the kind of clearcut physical confrontation that leaves a young man with a bodily feeling of strength and competence. In the second place it is not a new arena of competition but one which is all too familiar. Most adolescents want to match themselves against their contemporaries under circumstances different from what they have been used to in their home or school environment. They wish to be separated from the advantages that have been given them by the accident of birth or through the efforts of their parents or grandparents.

Unearned prestige and material aid from families which cannot sensibly be refused begin to chafe in the late teens, and a wish to be unencumbered by such things begins to emerge. This desire for a genuine test of strength and endurance remains unexpressed in many. Although a few drop out of school to demonstrate their independence by hitchhiking across the country, earning their way as they go, or putting to sea on a freighter, many more talk of it and would welcome permission or an invitation to do it by their parents or their school.

One pioneering answer to this problem of providing meaningful challenge to the young in these days of affluence is the organization called "Outward Bound Incorporated," which has founded three schools in this country to provide what their founder terms "authentic adventure" for boys from sixteen to twenty-three. The original Outward Bound school was started in Wales during World War II, when it was observed that older men exposed to many days at sea in lifeboats survived while the younger ones died, apparently because they gave up hope early and lost the will to live. In order to demonstrate to these young seamen what they were able to endure, a training experience was devised which stretched them close to the limit of physical tolerance. The results were so spectacular that the Outward Bound schools continued after the war, and affiliated schools were later started in Germany, Holland, and other countries.

In 1962 the first American Outward Bound School began putting its students through a truly challenging survival experience in Colorado. Now there are such schools in Minnesota and Maine, also. Training in rock-climbing, endurance swimming under adverse conditions, and a three-day solo experience in the wilderness with no creature comforts and a compulsory opportunity to learn how to live off the land are included. These adventures teach a boy things about himself he had no idea of before, and help him in a four-week period to respect himself more and to realize that courage and determination are part of his make-up.

Although the Outward Bound schools reach every economic group through their extensive scholarship program, only about a thousand boys each summer can profit from this program. This leaves hundreds of thousands without a similar opportunity to meet a challenge which can accurately and thoroughly test them. Unless this type of survival camp experience can be taken over by community or goverment organizations to enable many more to go through such training, some other way to accomplish these aims should be found.

One answer is required service in the Armed Forces—a draft that cannot be avoided because of marriage, schooling, or minor physical disability. The peacetime army does not provide a physically satisfying test of the limits of one's endurance in the way that the Outward Bound experience does. Its usefulness as a maturing event is more in the area of equalizing the encounter with peers, in such a way that promotions and awards are a result of true performance, uninfluenced by name or money. This matching against peers without artificial or accidental advantage leads to an increased sense of individual worth, as well as self-respect gained from honestly excelling or else successfully coping with the disappointment resulting from failure.

Required military service would work a hardship on those

who are strongly pacifist, and it might have unfortunate political implications in appearing to represent a military build-up.

An alternative to a universal military service program would be a required year of government service which could be taken at any time between the ages of eighteen and twenty-four. This could be work with the Peace Corps in foreign countries, or in domestic work of the same sort with government agencies such as VISTA or approved private ones. Those whose skills would not be useful in such organizations and who did not choose military service could spend a year instead in the Job Corps, learning a skill for later occupational use but at the same time going through an experience away from home which would involve the kind of physical and emotional challenge that characterizes the Outward Bound schools. Although Americans, generally speaking, are opposed to regimentation and compulsion of any sort, they might well be persuaded that this kind of testing experience for young people is as important to their healthy emotional development as being compelled to attend school until the age of sixteen.

Civil rights movements such as SNCC and CORE have occupied the time of many late adolescents, and for a few these organizations appear to be the answer to the need for challenge but useful and significant as this activity may be, it involves a very small proportion of the student population. While there is no doubt about the reality of the risk which is part of doing volunteer work in the South, the sporadic nature of most demonstrations and the loose-knit character of the coordinating agencies has an unstructured quality which usually fails to provide a maturing experience. The dedication and courage of the volunteers is admirable, but, for many, work in these movements has proved disruptive and shattering rather than constructive and integrating. This may be because of the original psychological make-up of the workers rather than the nature of the experience. It is too soon to tell.

Providing accurate information, setting a good example, and providing a challenge should be foremost in these times when most of us are capable of giving youth so much and challenges are so limited. Most important in providing these essentials, however, is a willingness on our part to try to understand and respond to the unspoken demands which stem from the young. These demands are for firmness, consistency, and respect from parents and teachers. The needs are so often covered over by belligerent requests for unlimited freedom, by expectations that we tolerate ridiculous extremes in behavior and dress, and by surly defiance, that we miss the message that lies beneath. We must learn to translate the language of the adolescent if we are to understand him. His true message is often the opposite of what his words and action seem immediately to imply. He tells us so often and so clearly to leave him alone when at heart he may want us to pay attention. The students at Berkeley were demanding freedom at one moment and asking for more personal interest from authority at the next. There is no way to achieve a permanent and total harmony between the generations, but in today's world there is wide room for improvement.

Index

Abortion, 51
Acne, 68
Addiction, 66-70, 73-74, 78, 134
Adoption, 51
Adultery, 130
Advanced placement, 101
Affluence, 1, 9, 11, 25, 36, 98
Albee, Edward, 130
Alcohol, 6, 16, 75, 79-80
Allport, Gordon, 115, 122
Amytal, 78
Antisocial behavior, 126
Apathy, 13, 69, 83, 101-105, 112
Armed Forces, 137
Athletics, 30, 117

Benzedrine, 66, 71, 78
Binger, Carl, 89
Boarding school, 19, 59
Bomb shelters, 12

Braiman, Alex, 95
Brandeis University, 96
Brewster, Kingman, 35, 96
British Columbia, University of, 100
Brown, Rev. H. O. J., 115, 125

Caffeine, 73
California, University of, 100
    at Berkeley, 92-95, 99, 110, 139
Cancer, 134
Carnegie Corporation, 35
Catholic Youth Organization, 117
Challenge, 11, 80, 128-139
Cheating, 105, 106
Church, 64, 101, 106, 114, 121, 126, 134
    dealing with rebellion, 117
    development of self-discipline, 3
    new morality, 124-125
    youth organizations, 117
Cigarettes, 65, 75, 114

141

INDEX

Civil disobedience, 89
Civil rights, 89, 93, 138
Cocaine, 73
Coeducation, 37, 39, 57, 109
Colby College, 29
Communism, 82, 106
Conscience, 59, 102, 123
 development of, 4-6, 10-14, 116
 dishonesty, 105-109
 obstacles to formation, 6-9
Contraception, 46, 47, 49
CORE, 138
Cortisone, 66
Crime, 6, 63
Curriculum, 38, 41, 47

Death, 17, 69, 79, 103, 109
Delinquency, 85, 119
DeMolay, 117
Depression, 31, 54, 109-113
 from drugs, 76, 78
 in children from divorce, 20, 23
Dexamyl, 78
Dexedrine, 78
Discipline, 7, 81, 106
 in early childhood, 8, 19
 in rebellion, 85
Dishonesty, 105-109, 112
 cheating, 105, 106
 plagiarizing, 105, 109
Divorce, 14-24
 boarding school, 19
 custody of children, 18-24
 depression of children, 20, 23
 effects of, 14-16
 rates of, 14, 52
Doors of Perception, The (Huxley), 77
Dropouts, 33-36
 rate at Harvard, 34
 Yale program, 35
Drugs, 65-80
 addiction, 66-70, 73-74, 78, 134
 China, 66
 Great Britain, 66
 motives for taking, 67-73
 withdrawal symptoms, 74

Eagle Scouts, 84
Early admissions, 100
Education, 25-42, 100, 109
 advanced placement, 101
 Carnegie Corporation, 35
 causes of underachievement, 27-33
 coeducation, 37, 39, 57, 109
 curriculum, 38, 41, 47
 dropouts, 33-36
 early admissions, 100
 examinations, 26
 "farm system," 40
 graduate school, 100, 101, 109
 in Europe, 25-26
 of women, 36-39
 sex, 43
 status motive, 28
 teaching machines, 8
Elliott, George P., 131, 133
Examinations, 26
Extramarital intercourse, 49, 51-52

Fanny Hill (Cleland), 132
Freud, Sigmund, 121-122
 concept of the unconscious, 118
 discipline, 7
 pleasure principle, 11
Friedan, Betty, 37
Frigidity, 7
Fry, Clements, 98
"Future of an Illusion, The" (Freud), 121-122

Goddard College, 39
Graduate school, 100, 101, 109
Guilt, 23, 106, 108
 from sex, 47, 60, 64

Hamilton College, 39
Hamlet, 45
Harper's Magazine, 131
Harvard University, 56, 99, 100, 122
 dropout rate, 34
 religious study, 115
Hemingway, Ernest, 102, 103
Hillel, 117
Hiroshima, 12

142

After receiving his A.B. from Harvard College in 1940 and his M.D. from Columbia College of Physicians and Surgeons in 1943, GRAHAM B. BLAINE, JR., served his internship and residency at Bellevue Hospital in New York City and at the Austen Riggs Foundation in Stockbridge, Massachusetts. His service as a medical officer in World War II was followed by three years of general practice in Kent, Connecticut, a year of private psychiatric practice in New York, and work on the staffs of Riggs Clinic and Williams College. Dr. Blaine joined the Harvard University Health Services in 1955, and has been their chief of psychiatry since 1964. In addition to treating the emotional difficulties of Harvard and Radcliffe graduate and undergraduate students, he is involved with the problems of younger adolescents at the Children's Hospital in Boston. He is the author of *Patience and Fortitude: The Parent's Guide to Adolescence*, co-author (with Charles C. McArthur) of *Emotional Problems of the Student*, and has written numerous articles.

Dr. Blaine and his wife live in Cambridge with their three daughters.